A SWARTHY BOY

By the same author:

Previously published:

CORENTYNE THUNDER
A MORNING AT THE OFFICE
SHADOWS MOVE AMONG THEM
CHILDREN OF KAYWANA
THE WEATHER IN MIDDENSHOT
THE LIFE AND DEATH OF SYLVIA
THE HARROWING OF HUBERTUS
MY BONES AND MY FLUTE
OF TREES AND THE SEA
A TALE OF THREE PLACES
KAYWANA BLOOD
THE WEATHER FAMILY
A TINKLING IN THE TWILIGHT
LATTICED ECHOES
ELTONSBRODY
THUNDER RETURNING
THE MAD MACMULLOCHS
THE PILING OF CLOUDS
THE WOUNDED AND THE WORRIED

Non-fiction

WITH A CARIB EYE

PLATE I A swarthy boy—scowling at the camera because he was forced to wear an effeminate silk bow instead of a tie (see Page 55)

A SWARTHY BOY

by

Edgar Mittelholzer

PUTNAM
GREAT RUSSELL STREET
LONDON

First Published in Great Britain in 1963 by
PUTNAM & COMPANY LIMITED
42 Great Russell Street · London · WC1
and printed by
Ebenezer Baylis and Son Limited
The Trinity Press · Worcester and London

CONTENTS

LIST OF ILLUSTRATIONS

A SWARTHY BOY

Chapter One

BACKGROUND

BECAUSE OF the damp—the humidity is excessively high—and the low, swampy nature of the land, virtually every dwelling-place in British Guiana stands on pillars: pillars either of wood or of bricks, and generally about ten feet tall. The Lutheran Manse in New Amsterdam was no exception. Its pillars were of brick, and it was a large, spreading two-storied wooden building painted white. It may be—and may look—exactly the same to-day; I haven't seen it for more than twenty years. The church that stood nearby was also painted white and was also wooden built. In the last two decades of the nineteenth century and the first decade of the present century, when my grandfather, the pastor, and his family lived in the manse, the church was already well over a hundred years old. It was built by the Dutch (who first owned and governed British Guiana before the British came) in 1744.

New Amsterdam is a little town at the mouth of the Berbice River, on the eastern side of the two-and-a-quarter-mile-wide estuary, at least eight miles from the plantation up-river where, during the early part of the nineteenth century, Jan Vincent Mittelholzer, my great-grandfather, was manager over some few hundred acres of sugar-canes and the negro slaves who worked on the land.

Much further up-river, over fifty miles from the estuary, Plantation de Vreede, flourishing in the middle of the eighteenth century, had, even before the nineteenth century began, reverted to the jungle from which it had been won. In 1760, with its neighbours—plantations with such names as Peereboom, Hollandia, Lilienburg, Oosterbeck and Doorn-boom—Plantation de Vreede swarmed with activity, and ships came up-river to bring supplies from Europe and take away the produce. The manager of Plantation de Vreede was a Swiss-German, Herr C. Mittelholzer, the first Mittelholzer, so far as anyone knows, to come to this part of the world. He came from the canton of Geneva, but was probably born in Appenzell which is the original home of the family. There are two districts in Appenzell where the family was firmly established as far back as the early seventeenth century—Rämsen and Mittelholz. According to what I was told by the present head of the family in Appenzell, Dr. Johann Mittelholzer, a veterinary surgeon, the Mittelholzers were always gipsy-like in their tendencies. They not only drifted about in their own Switzerland but drifted away to other countries.

On a visit to Appenzell, my wife and I were shown a large ledger-like book whose yellowed pages were filled with microscopic black German words in a neat, sloping script. Between the two tough, thick, age-grey covers there could easily have been the text of three full-length novels. My kinsman admitted that he had never been able to decipher it all. He assured me, however, that it appeared to be a record of life on a plantation in one of the former Dutch colonies in South America. About 1886, he said, it had suddenly appeared in Switzerland, sent to his father by someone unknown overseas on behalf of a recently deceased member of the Mittelholzer family. There was no letter accompanying it: only a large, heavy silver spoon, which he also showed us.

I have always wondered what the "C" stood for in the name of this mid-eighteenth century Mittelholzer—assuming that the record was his—and as a result of my visit to Appenzell, I think I have, at last, been able to get on the track of something definite.

Dr. Johann Mittelholzer, at seventy-eight, is as active and bristlingly alert as a man thirty or forty years his junior, and his interest in family history is extremely keen. In fact, his whole family is keen on the subject. Shortly after my visit he wrote me to say that his eldest daughter, because of the interest I showed in the old ledger from South America, had spent the whole Whitsuntide week-end probing into the miniscule script. To quote: "*Den ganzen Tag blättert sie herum und findet eine ganze Reihe Notizen von mehreren Mittelholzer aus dem 18. Jahrhundert und in dieser Zeit war bei den männlichen der*

Vorname Constanz und bei den weiblichen Constantine sehr beliebt und nun erinnere ich mich auch, in meiner kleinen Münzsammlung einen sogenannten Tauftaler zu haben auf dem eingeprägt ist: Patin Constatia Mittelholzer."

It seems very likely, then, that the "C" in the name of my ancestor who managed Plantation de Vreede stood for Constanz. And if the "so-called baptismal coin" is to be believed, his godmother must have been called Constatia. Perhaps she was a dear old aunt, the feminine name-equivalent of the traditional masculine Constanz.

Apart from this ledger and silver spoon, the only other relic from the eighteenth century that I know of is a sabre (my father called it a scimitar whenever he spoke of it). About thirty years ago I saw it in the home of my Uncle John in Georgetown, hanging on the wall in a dark corner. It has since been passed down to his eldest son, my first cousin, Frank.

The story is that our ancestor used this sabre to defend himself against the negro slaves when he was a fugitive in the jungle during the savage and bloody slave insurrection of 1763. He is reputed to have hacked off the hand of at least one of his attackers and laid out a number of others before eventually winning his way to safety. He had been one of thirty whites besieged in the church-house at Plantation Peereboom and had escaped being shot down by jumping into the river and swimming off.

There can be no doubt that it was Jan Vincent on his plantation eight miles up-river who, in the early part of the nineteenth century, dropped the pebble that started the ripple of black blood in the family. I have seen a photograph of him, and the picture was clear enough to show that he was pure European, even clear enough to show that he had suffered some injury to one of his eyes. The aunt who showed me the picture (in a huge family-album) told me that he had been chasing a slave guilty of some misdemeanour when he fell and sustained this injury.

My grandfather, John Robert, the Lutheran pastor, was definitely a man of colour. He had an olive complexion, and features that revealed his admixture; also, his hair, while not frizzy like a negro's, was far too curly and dark to be entirely

European. Even though I was not yet four when he died, I can remember him quite clearly. He had a black beard and dark-brown, gentle eyes. He was a man of medium height, portly and paunched.

It was not until a long time afterwards, however, that I came to know anything about him. It was he who had founded a little church for the aboriginal Indians, about ninety miles up the Berbice River, at a place called Maria Henrietta which he visited periodically; it was run permanently by a resident "catechist", as he was called. My grandfather was a man well versed in Latin, Greek, Hebrew and German, and, in his spare-time, painted in oils. He also kept in the manse, during the week, a small private-school exclusively for the sons of the gentlemen of the town. He called it Geneva Academy.

I doubt whether there could have been more than twenty pupils, for it was a small town of six or seven thousand of whom probably more than ninety-eight per cent were non-gentlemen. The gentlemen were the merchants, book-keepers, parsons, doctors, senior Civil Servants and those planters who had town houses, and these were white, near-white, and olive-complexioned admixtures. Negroes—the men of pure African blood—had not yet qualified as gentlemen. They were still exclusively shoemakers, carpenters, postmen, tin-smiths, gardeners, policemen, coachmen and, of course, domestic servants.

Life in the homes of Guiana gentlemen was as severely Victorian as in the homes of gentlemen in England at the same period. The dress was the same; the fact that the climate was hot made no difference. Only the planters on their plantations, and their overseers, dispensed with collars and ties and condescended to wear white drill during the day. In town, the merchants and the book-keepers, the parsons and the doctors and the senior Civil Servants, morning and evening, dressed as their counterparts in Surrey and Essex dressed in the summer at that period. Ladies vied with each other to be fashionably garbed, just as ladies in Cheltenham or in Tunbridge Wells were doing four thousand miles away. Young gentlemen asked permission to visit the homes of the young women for whom they took a fancy. Flowers spoke a language for lovers. Sex was an unpleasant rumour that seldom, and only accidentally, penetrated into respectable drawing-rooms (note, drawing-rooms; no respectable gentleman or lady of Guiana would speak of a sitting- or living-room!).

In the drawing-room of the Lutheran Manse sex had never been heard of—not even in the form of a rumour. Even more so than the other respectable homes, the home of the Lutheran pastor had to be a place of unsullied propriety.

It was in such an atmosphere that my father and his brothers and sisters grew up. There were seven of them—John, Elfreda, William (my father), Louise, Jane, Albert and Anna. The girls, no doubt, attended some *very* private school (fifteen or twenty pupils) for the daughters of gentlemen, but the boys were taught by their father at home along with the other pupils of Geneva Academy.

The three boys and two of the girls, Elfreda and Louise, herited the talent for drawing and painting that both their parents possessed. My paternal grandmother (her name was Jane) died long before I was born, but I have seen one or two of her drawings and paintings, as I have done some of the work of my grandfather and uncles and aunts. Nothing startling. Very conventional, Academy sort of art that featured much representational detail and careful drawing.

Of them all, my Uncle John was the only one with a truly adventurous spirit. By this I mean that he had not only enough courage to leave the Lutheran Church when he came of age and join the Roman Catholic Church but also to brave the black contumely of the small-town Victorian society in which he lived by leading the life of a roué (even if his activities were of a *sub rosa* kind in keeping with the gentlemanly code of those days). He fathered at least one illegitimate child, a son, that I know of, and who even adopted his name. Through the influence of my grandfather, Uncle John got into the Civil Service, and rose rapidly, eventually retiring as Comptroller of Customs. He served as Mayor of New Amsterdam on two occasions. He was an architect in his spare time, and designed several buildings in Georgetown, including St. Stanislaus' College, the Roman Catholic secondary school for boys. In addition, he took an interest in the local military, and was commissioned a major in the Artillery.

Albert (Uncle Bertie, as he was called not only by his

nephews and nieces but affectionately by old and young people of his acquaintance) was a shy, self-effacing man and a figure of fun wherever he went—a sort of Chekhov character. He was a dreamy man who blushed at the mere mention of women. He never married, but I heard on good authority that he wrote many a love-letter to many a lady—but kept them in a drawer instead of sending them to the ladies to whom they were addressed. He was very pale in complexion, with pale-blue eyes whose irises never touched the line of the lower lid, thus emphasising his dreamy expression. I myself often teased him about his getting married, and he always turned a bright red, quivered with self-conscious chuckles and insisted in his thin, high-pitched voice: "Oh, yes! I intend to get married. Wait and you'll see. Just you wait." He was an excellent draughtsman, especially of faces. And he was clever at making toys. He once made me a perfect little launch that could sail under its own power, the propeller being worked by strips of rubber wound taut and then released. He, too, entered the Civil Service, but so lacking in concentration was he—so dreamy and indolent during office hours; he wrote little love-poems, I have heard, instead of writing up his ledgers in the Department of Registry and Deeds—that he was made to retire at the age of forty-five. He remained a staunch member of the Lutheran Church until his death.

My father was a shy and self-effacing young man, too. Right into middle-age, in fact. And he was dreamy—but in somewhat different fashion, compared with his brother. He was a scheming dreamer, and his big dream was to travel to England and Europe. Again through the influence of my grandfather who was friendly with Sir H.K.D., the principal of a big merchant firm in the town, my father became a clerk in the head-office of this firm, and got on very well. He certainly did not while away his time writing love-poems in office-hours. And in 1901 he realised his dream. He had saved enough to travel to England and Europe. He spent the summer months of that year in London, Paris and Switzerland. He wrote a long account of this trip which still exists, neatly typewritten and bound, with a small water-colour sketch of Lake Geneva done by himself on the cover. His literary style, as in everything he has written—short stories and letters to the Press—was

Gibbon-like and sonorous, and lavishly besprinkled with Latin phrases; he has always had a weakness for Latin phrases.

Despite his shyness, he was fond of ballroom dancing—the Caledonian, Lancers, the waltz and the other dances of his day—and at one time (it took me a lot to believe *this*!) even acted as master of ceremonies at various balls. Also, he evidently had the courage, like his elder brother, to switch to the church of his choice. When he came of age he left the Lutheran Church and got confirmed in the Church of England.

I often wonder how the Lutheran pastor reacted to these defections on the part of his sons. Did he just take it in a spirit of calm, charitable Christian philosophy! I have heard it said that he was a man of imperturbable temperament, and the suggestion is that he lived in a scholarly dream-world. Walking on the street, he stared before him in theological abstraction, and always had to be greeted first. He and Bishop Austin, the head of the Anglican diocese in Guiana, had for many years been close friends—there is a portrait of the Bishop done by my grandfather which used to hang in my aunts' home—and it was indirectly through this friendship that, ironically, my father acquired a strong liking for the Church of England. In fact, my father's Christian names are William Austin; the Pastor had named him after the Bishop.

On the 20th of January, 1909, William Austin, at the age of thirty-four, married Rosamond Mabel, youngest daughter of David Leblanc. She was twenty.

David Leblanc was brought to British Guiana as a small boy. He came of a French creole family in Martinique. Very handsome, decidedly Gallic in tendencies, yet English in voice and deportment, he was a ladies' man all his life—but in the Victorian manner: under cover of gentlemanly discretion. He began humbly. At the age of seventeen he was taken on as a telegraph clerk in the Post Office. But he had ability and charm, and rose very quickly, eventually retiring as Acting Postmaster General. He had a wide circle of friends in both Georgetown and New Amsterdam.

His wife, my maternal grandmother, was a Downer—Rebecca Downer—daughter of a Lancashire man who owned and ran what was known as a cooperage, in the eastern part of the town; evidently a cask- and vat-making concern of some sort. The street called Cooper's Lane in New Amsterdam was named after his cooperage. He was a staunch member of the Congregationalist Church, and his son William became a Congregationalist minister. My grandmother sang in the choir, was a Sunday-school teacher and arranged what were known as "soirées" for the church-members, a form of very innocuous social entertainment that apparently encompassed "a sale of work" in aid of a new harmonium or repairs to the manse. She was not fervently, but perfervidly, religious—yet also very feminine. Feminine enough to succumb to the charms of David Leblanc despite his worldly and non-religious outlook.

From the outset, however, it must have been obvious that theirs would not be the ideal marriage. I had a very keen ear as a boy, and even though the discussion of intimate matters was taboo before children, I was able to gather that my grandfather, in spite of an impeccable outward respectability (he had four daughters, and they all held him in high esteem), was far too gay a lad with the ladies to suit my grandmother's Congregationalist soul. I can remember hearing her (I was about ten) narrating an anecdote to a close friend—this very late in her life by which time she had forgiven if not forgotten—and in the course of it she said: "My dear child, I waited up until he came in, and I faced him and told him what I'd heard. I said: 'But, David, aren't you ashamed of yourself! *Three* in one night!' "

The chuckling, affectionate sigh of reminiscence that followed was, I am sure, no indication of how she must have reacted at the time of these escapades, for she was no tame, docile Christian wife. She was a dynamic personality, dramatic—indeed, often melodramatic—in voice and manner.

Inevitably came the break. A year or two before I was born —or perhaps just about that time; I won't be positive—my grandfather left her to go and live on his own.

Chapter Two

A SWARTHY BABY

LUTHERAN COURT is an oblong strip of land about five acres in extent that runs east-west between the two main thoroughfares in New Amsterdam—Main Street (officially High Street) and the Strand, which is the chief business street. The church and the manse are situated at the western end. At the extreme eastern end, that is on Main Street, stood —and, I believe, still stands—a two-storied cottage, the property of the Lutheran Church. It was in this cottage that my parents first lived when they got married, and it was here that I was born at 2 a.m. on the sixteenth of December, 1909.

For my father, it was an occasion of momentous disappointment. I turned out a swarthy baby!

Himself fair-complexioned with hair of European texture, as were his brothers and sisters (save Anna, the youngest), and his wife also fair-complexioned and European in appearance, he had, naturally, assumed that the chances were heavy in favour of a fair-complexioned baby. (Widely read in his teens and as a young man, had he, I wonder, heard of Mendelism?). However, there it was. His first-born—a swarthy boy!

Always a confirmed negrophobe, he must have felt it deeply that December morning. He has my empathy. It requires the minimum of effort for me to put myself in his place. In a community like that, at that time, he would have had to be superhuman not to be disappointed. A bleak morning and a sunny, dry afternoon: such is the analogy of contrast that could be applied to a swarthy and a fair complexion[1] in New Amsterdam in the year 1909.

There was one important consolation for him, though. I

[1] *See* Appendix 1.

stress important. My hair was dead straight. No sign of any negroid kinks.

Could they have foreseen what my attitude towards orthodox religion was to be in my twenties, my parents might have hesitated before choosing for me the names Edgar Austin. My father and mother were members of All Saints Church, the parish church, and the Rector, an Englishman, evidently did not mind my swarthiness. He it was, in fact, on one of his visits to the home, who insisted that I should be named after him. And it was he, the Reverend Mr. Edgar Josa,[1] who baptized me. I have always thought it ironical, in view of my rejection of conventional Christianity and adoption of Yoga and Oriental Occultism, that I should have been named after a Church of England priest and (obliquely) a bishop.

My earliest memory goes back to when I was only a year old. My parents were astounded that I could have remembered it, but in my teens I told them of how I recalled yelling in a frenzy of fright in the big double bed in the room on the Main Street side of the cottage whenever a certain toy was put into operation beside me. It was a German toy and consisted of a cart and a donkey. When wound up and put down, the donkey pranced wildly, pulling the cart after it. It was this prancing that terrified me. My mother had to agree that this actually happened. It was no fantasy of mine.

Another very clear and vivid memory—though for obvious reasons I have never asked them to confirm it—is of my nurse, a shapely negro girl, seated on a large travelling trunk in the corridor outside the big bedroom, with me in her lap, casually fumbling out a full breast and letting me fondle it. I'm sure this happened more than once, and I'm equally sure that on one occasion my father passed us, on his way from the bedroom to the stairway, but pretended not to notice. (The picture of this incident, in particular, is too clear in my mind to have been something just imagined up in later years.) It must have been my earliest erotic experience which probably explains why I remember it so distinctly.

Yet equally as vivid is the picture of myself being held in the arms of this or another nurse at the pantry window on the southern side of the cottage. From this window we could look

[1] Pronounced Yohzah.

straight into the open doorway—the north-eastern entrance—of All Saints Church, not more than a hundred yards distant in Church Street. I can see at this moment the pendant cluster of electric lights glittering over the pews, and recall the feeling of anxiety I had because of the knowledge that both my father and mother were at Evensong and I was alone with the nurse at home. I kept asking her when they would come home, and she kept assuring me: "As soon as church over."

Then there was the blackened patch on one of the bedroom doors caused by some clothes hanging on pegs catching fire one evening. My father was in time to put out the blaze before it could spread and take hold. I have no memory of the actual incident but was told about it after it had occurred. I must have been very curious on seeing the paint-scorched door and I probably asked questions. My Great-aunt Mary, my maternal grandmother's sister, it appears, had been spending time with us, and it was her clothes that had caught fire. There had been some carelessness involving a flat iron in a coal-pot (a receptacle for holding glowing coal).

My sister was born in February, 1911, but the event did not register on me. I can remember her only as a toddler. She was fair-complexioned.

Meantime, there was a change of residence. My father was transferred to Georgetown, and we lived in another two-storied place in a street called Robb Street. The cottage was owned by a Mr. Lopes, a Portuguese, and it seems that here I entered a destructive phase. I distinctly remember an occasion when I took up some glass object—a tumbler or a mug—from a dinner-wagon and hurled it through the kitchen door, chortling in delight at the tinkling crash it made as it disintegrated on the ground. My mother has related to friends what a menace I was to the glassware in the house.

Just one other memory I have of this Georgetown cottage. It was of a large frog hopping off in the back-yard under the tall breadfruit tree and the cook hurrying out with a jar of salt. She kept sprinkling salt on its back to the accompaniment of loud shrieks of laughter until eventually my mother came downstairs to find out what the hullabaloo was about.

They say infants are psychic. Perhaps, without being aware

of it, I saw many a robust ghost in this cottage, for I heard that it was haunted. My mother was nervous to live in it, but she had to admit that she never saw anything spectral while we were there. However, it seems that there must have been something odd about the place, because at the very end, when we were leaving, a manifestation occurred. My father, an arch-sceptic, was alone downstairs in the drawing-room awaiting the arrival of the men who were going to take away the furniture, covered and stacked together upstairs, when he heard a terrific thumping and crashing in one of the bedrooms. He hurried upstairs, expecting to see that some wash-stand, perhaps, with its earthenware mug, wash-basin and soap-dishes, had collapsed, or perhaps that some animal had found its way upstairs and had gone berserk. But the instant he got upstairs the noise ceased—and when he looked round, everything was precisely as he had left it a short while before, intact and untouched. Puzzled, he returned downstairs—and almost at once the pandemonium started again.

In spite of this, however, he continued to be an arch-sceptic. He always pooh-pooh-ed supernatural phenomena.

I cannot say definitely, but I have an idea we went back to the cottage in Lutheran Court. What I know for certain is that there were quarrels between my parents—quarrels that generally ended by my mother bursting into tears. This spectacle always moved me deeply. It created in me a feeling of catastrophe, and I never failed to weep in sympathy.

What comes back very portentously are the visits to the manse.

These occurred in the afternoon, and my father usually took me, though sometimes the nurse came along, too. I see them in retrospect as Ordeals of the first magnitude.

There was my grandfather—the Parson, as everyone called him—bending down to kiss me. His black beard awed me. And it had a scent of its own. Was it of ginger or a cross between ginger and talcum powder? His eyes were kindly, gentle and humorous, but I was always tense in his presence. And this tension was probably increased by the presence of my father whom I feared. Even at this green age, I could sense a certain resentment in his attitude towards me. Then, naturally, I was ignorant of what was behind it. All I knew was that something made him perpetually impatient with me. Something made it necessary for him to snap and bark at me.

Whenever in the manse, he seemed to go out of his way to try to demonstrate what I can only describe as the "compensatory" side of me. I can almost hear him thinking behind scowls: "Oh, well, he may be dark-skinned, but he does seem to have some intelligence". These demonstrations would take the form of quizzes. He would ask me questions before my grandfather and aunts in order to hear me give the correct answers.

But there came the afternoon when I let him down.

As clearly as though it happened the day before yesterday, I can see myself, a small boy of three, standing beside my grandfather's bed upstairs in the manse. My grandfather was bedridden at the time. My father quizzed me as usual, and I managed to answer correctly the first two or three questions. Then he leant towards me and asked: "And now tell Grandpa —what is the young of a sheep called?"

"A calf," I replied.

"Don't be silly!" barked my father. "What is the young of a *sheep* called? A *sheep*!"

I began to throw baffled, desperate glances about me.

"Come on, come on! Speak up!"

"I don't know," I murmured.

"You do know. Come on. What is the young of a sheep called?"

"A goat," I stammered, shaking.

My father bellowed at me. My grandfather remonstrated at him in a low voice from the bed. I began to howl. But this only spurred my father to sterner action. He grabbed me by the arm and hauled me off downstairs to the study. In there, he bent low, his face red and angry, and bawled at me: "What is the young of a sheep called, you little fool?"

I tried to stammer out an answer through my blubbering, but it was still the wrong one.

"What is the young of a sheep called?" bellowed my father, and he danced in his rage. No cliché. No exaggeration. His feet always moved agitatedly when he was enraged.

Abruptly Aunt Carrie came to the rescue. Her name was Caroline Fraser, and she was a thin, small person. She was related in some way to Uncle John's wife. She lived in the manse with my real aunts and kept house. Her eyes spurted fury as she drew me protectively against her skirt. I can hear her outraged voice as she said to my father: "Aren't you ashamed of yourself, Willy? He's only a child."

"He's a little fool!" shouted my father, stamping. And undaunted, he bent down towards me and bellowed: "What is the young of a sheep called?"

"Yah-ow!" I yelled, clutching at Aunt Carrie's skirt.

"What is the young of a sheep called?"

Aunt Carrie's head came low, and she murmured: "A lamb, dear."

Then she turned again upon my father and counter-attacked in my defence. It was a painful, rather ugly—for me, utterly terrifying—scene.

There is another aspect of terror associated with the manse. Elvira.

She was the cook—a negress with cross eyes. She would appear suddenly just before I was taken upstairs to see my grandfather—she probably opened the door for my father or the nurse, if I happened to have been brought by the nurse—and she would say something to me, her eyes rolling fantastically. I would recoil and whimper, shuddering and wriggling in fright.

Probably at first she did not intend to produce this effect, but later, I am sure, realising the power of her eyes over me, she used to do it on purpose. I can remember, even at home, my nurse threatening, when I was naughty, to take me to Elvira if I did not behave myself. Ever since those days, the name Elvira has lurked in my imagination, a symbol of evil. I could not possibly name a character Elvira in one of my novels unless I depicted her as someone sinister.

It can be frustrating to try disentangling the events of one's early childhood. Individual incidents loom up with clarity, but you can never be sure which came before the other. I know that these visits to my grandfather took place before my fourth birthday, because I know that my grandfather died during the year 1913, but did they occur before or after (or before *and* after) my father lost his job at S.D. & Co.?

One of his colleagues in the office was a certain Angus

Fraser, of the Fraser family into which my Uncle John had married, and it appears that Uncle Angus (that's what I used to call him when I got to know him a few years later) had been indulging in a number of book-keeping acrobatics—called in newspaper reports "defalcations". There must even have been "embezzlement" as well. Anyway, my father discovered these defalcations, was horrified, but, not wanting to get Uncle Angus into trouble, kept silent. Foolish of him, for he must have realised that Uncle Angus could not get away with it for ever. Inevitably came the exposure. The chopper fell on Uncle Angus, with a side-swipe for my father who was blamed for not reporting the irregularities the moment he had discovered them.

My mother has often spoken—and spoken with great bitterness—of what she had to endure during that year or more when my father was out of work. He took it badly. He has always had a great sense of responsibility, and I can well imagine the agonies he must have suffered.

My maternal grandmother, who lived with her two daughters (my Aunt Bertha and Aunt Maud) in a cottage in Coburg Street, suggested that we should come and live with her until the situation improved. It must have been hurtful to my father's pride, but he agreed, and we moved in on my grandmother. Moved in, as it happened, to stay.

Chapter Three

COBURG STREET

I HAVE BEEN using the word "cottage". Living in England is responsible for this. It is a kind of heresy on my part. In British Guiana, no respectable middle-class family would be heard talking about the cottage in which they lived. No matter how modest it is, of one storey or two, of three rooms or six, a cottage is a house. Only the lower classes live in cottages.

My brothers and sister would blink at me if I spoke to them of "the Coburg Street cottage", because we are accustomed to referring to it as "the Coburg Street house". Yet it is only of one storey. When my parents, with my sister and myself, moved in, it consisted of a drawing-room (*sic*) and dining-room and three bedrooms, with two servants' rooms on the ground-floor (bottom-house) section-level. This, I am aware, is a little difficult to convey to any-one who has never lived in Guiana. Imagine the house standing on its ten-foot wooden pillars. You can walk quite freely and erect *under* the house, and this area is called the bottom-house. Then imagine a specified space between the pillars being boarded in and floored—and there are your servants' rooms.

Further, imagine a stairway *outside* the building leading up from the gateway to the small portico, this stairway for visitors and the postman, and another stairway leading up to the kitchen at the back for tradesmen and servants. Imagine, also, about an acre and a half of grounds—the Yard, we called it; front-yard and back-yard. The front-yard was planted with crotons and flowering shrubs, the back-yard with a variety of fruit trees—mango, guava, star-apple, custard-apple, shaddock (a citrus fruit much like grapefruit) and one or two cactus plants. Also there was a brick oven standing on stilts, all by itself, not far from the kitchen; cake and bread were baked in it. Near the fence, right at the back of the back-yard, stood the rickety latrine for the servants.

To the west of us, in about three acres of grounds, stood the two-storied house of our neighbours, the Luckhoos, an East Indian family. To the east of us, in about an acre of grounds, stood another two-storied place. Here lived the Eggs, a near-white family. Mr. Tyrer Egg was a solicitor, and his son Richard (Dicky to my mother and aunts) was also plodding on a legal path. He became a barrister and eventually a judge.

Directly opposite our house, imposing and adding social prestige to all the residents of Coburg Street (West), were the spacious grounds of the Central Police Station, with barracks, fire-station and Inspector's house contained therein. In the middle of a small gravel court separating the station and barracks building from the fire-station shed stood a huge, ancient sandbox tree with massive trunk and spreading foliage that rustled perpetually in the wind. To the west of the barracks, near the large, red iron water-storage tanks close up against the Inspector's residence, grew a smooth-trunked, perfectly straight cabbage palm. All cabbage palms are smooth-trunked and straight—military trees—and the one that grew not twenty yards from our drawing-room windows, just within the grounds of the Luckhoos' place, was no exception.

A seven-foot-tall corrugated iron fence bordered the grounds of the police station, from the Inspector's house to the fire-station, and passers-by could not see the smooth, green lawn that was used as a miniature parade ground.

In those days, the police force took the military side of their occupation seriously. A sentry, armed with rifle and fixed bayonet, kept duty at the entrance. The guard was changed with barked commands and much clicking of heels and sloping and ordering of arms. Every morning at five, the Reveille was sounded by a bugler, and at ten o'clock at night, the Last Post. To-day I can hum or tra-la any of those bugle-calls from beginning to end, without omitting a single note. Besides the Reveille and the Last Post, there was the one at six o'clock in the evening, and at a quarter to eight, and the Lights Out at a quarter past ten.

It was not until 1915—somehow, the year has stuck in my memory—that my grandmother decided to have electric current installed. Before that the house was lit by oil-lamps—ornate, white-shaded lamps pendant from the rafters. Yes, the rafters. Ceilings are rare in one-storied houses in Guiana. Because of the hot climate, there is an opening under the eaves to let in air. The walls dividing the various rooms rise to as high as where a ceiling ought to be. But instead of a ceiling, the whole roof space is left open so that currents of air can move unhindered between eaves and thus contribute to the coolness indoors.

Ours was one vast roof that sheltered everything; only the portico and the kitchen and pantry had separate roofs, and these were like after-thoughts that had been sprouted during an emergency. Considerable improvements and additions were made—in 1915—but this is what the Coburg Street place looked like when we moved into it in 1913.

Even if I had not been an impressionable child, I would have been awed by the great inverted V of gloom up in that roof. When I looked up, it was as though I were gazing at an uncharted sky of cross-beams and alternate laths and shingle-sections—it was a shingled roof, at first—and dangling tendrils of cobweb and the dark holes in rosettes of webs spun by the spider population added to the mystery and remote terrors high up there. It was a thrilling moment when, as happened periodically, especially at Christmas, my grandmother and the servants embarked on a cobwebbing session. The total length of the cobweb-broom, after the sections of handle had been fitted together, was about twenty feet, and my sister and I would huddle together in an excited group, gazing upwards at the furry black blob daringly poking about in the lofty twilight, destroying the rosettes of web and sometimes bringing down, in leisurely parachute fashion, some ugly black lump of curled legs—a spider jerked from its dusty, lamp-black crevice amidst the thousands of other lamp-black crevices far up there.

The drawing-room—it could not have been more than fifteen feet by twelve—was a jungle of furniture. And pictures. There was the centre-table, a round mahogany thing with carved legs, too Victorian to be true, and on this, like a holy pale-blue ghost, stood (I am tempted to say hovered) the Epergne. It was a complicated glass object composed of a delicate funnel-shaped vase in the middle surrounded by other smaller funnels that *hung* on even more delicately fashioned looped stems of glass. My sister and I were warned against approaching anywhere near it. The impression left on us by these warning voices was that should the Epergne ever be broken, the whole dark roof would cave in upon us in a roar of anger and reproof.

Not far from the centre table, in the south-western corner, loomed, black and untouchable, the upright Pohlmann piano. On the northern wall hung the Magic Mantelpiece—actually it was screwed on to the wall—and on it rested vases and glass ornaments, all duplicated in the bevelled oblongs of mirror that were a striking feature of the whole frail, dark structure of shelves and thin, carved columns and knobs.

In the south-eastern corner, like a mathematical problem, stood a tripod composed of three thick bamboos, polished—and probably stained—to look as furniture should look. These bamboos supported a square of wood, and on this square of wood stood the jardinière, an earthenware one in which at all times was kept a dense mass of croton cuttings, the dark reds and yellows and browns of the large leaves matching the colours and pattern of the jardinière itself.

Inserted in the remaining space were mahogany rocking chairs, occasional tables and upright chairs. All the chairs were draped with antimacassers which, white at Christmas, gradually grew yellow with dust as the new year advanced, then white again when they were changed at Easter.

From the walls large and small pictures in black and brown frames stared darkly at the furniture—reproductions of Lord Leighton's classical-sentimental Victorian masterpieces, a picture depicting Nelson as a boy, one called *The Rosary* showing a woman with a very soulful face, hands clasped, and light from heaven streaming down upon her, and various photographs—one of my grandfather, another of my grandmother, another of my Aunt Bertha in Edwardian finery, elbow on table with family-album. And I remember an oblong mirror in a black frame.

The carpet was an Axminster.

The sacred object in the dining-room was the dinner-wagon. It glittered with glassware, and Children Must Not Run Past It. On its top section—there were three sections—a dark-green glass jug always fascinated me. All through my childhood I used to wonder what it would be like to peer into it and see right down to the bottom. I was sure some wonderful shining treasure lurked in there, because my parents and grandmother and aunts were fond of putting things into the jugs for safety—well out of the reach of mischievous childish hands.

The pictures in the dining-room were not numerous, but the two that dominated the scene outshone in impressiveness anything to be found in the drawing-room. They faced each other on opposite walls—two huge black-framed lithographs of Gustav Doré's *The Vale of Tears* and *Christ Leaving the Praetorium*.

The dining-table was the least sacred item of furniture. My sister and I were allowed to sit under it to play when it was not in use. Here we shuffled about our toys and talked baby-talk and pretended we were grown-ups planning to keep house—and then suddenly disagreeing and fighting.

In these days I did not feel like a boy, and it was because my mother treated me with a sentimentality peculiarly her own. First of all, she felt that she had to protect me against my father's impatience; I was the Dark One at whom he was always frowning and barking. Secondly, she was very feminine and just could not help being fonder of me than of my sister—though she denied this emphatically when challenged. Thirdly, like my father himself, she was enough of a negrophobe to treasure my dead-straight European-texture hair. The result was that she let my hair grow long right to my waist like a girl's so that she could show me off to her friends. My sister and I frolicked around with long dark pigtails, and a stranger could easily have mistaken us both for girls. When, in my twenties, I reminded my mother, during a bitter quarrel, of this circumstance, she denied that she had ever allowed my hair to grow long like a girl's. Even when I pointed to a photograph of my sister and myself in her bedroom that showed me with a long plait coiled up on my head, she refused to admit it, trying to make out that it was only the way she had combed my hair. But her gaze avoided mine when she said this, because the photograph was too clear to be ignored.

Of David Leblanc's four daughters, my mother seemed to have been the most naïve, guileless and sentimental. My Aunt Irene died before I was born—in 1905, I believe—but from what I have heard, she must have been a far more sophisticated and practical person, allowing, of course, for the stress and strain of Victorian discipline. My Aunt Bertha, the eldest, was sentimental, but by no means naïve or guileless. Aunt Maud, though she never married, always had an air of confidence and sophistication, and sentiment she kept severely under control. I can't swear to it, but I feel that she must have been aware of the processes of Nature in her late teens, if not before, despite the ramparts of Victorian respectability that rigidly protected her and her sisters from the faintest rumour of sex. So, too, my Aunt Bertha. In some way, at some time, the Enemy must have infiltrated the defences, and messages of the Ugly World outside must have reached her ears. Not my mother, though. She has said it more than once. She knew absolutely nothing of sex when she married my father, and it came to her as a shock when she discovered on her wedding-night what was expected of her. My grandmother, she said, had made a rule that she and her sisters had to be indoors not one minute later than six every evening—twilight gathers at six every evening, all the year round, in Guiana—and even as a girl in her teens she trembled at the thought of arriving home after six. She has told, too, of the occasion when Dicky Egg of nextdoor happened to hold her in conversation at the gateway one afternoon. Six struck, but she did not realise it, and continued to chat to Dicky. Suddenly, the voice of her mother, like a bugle-blast, came from the portico. "Rosa! It is ten past six! Come in at once!" With a gasp, the seventeen-year-old Rosamond asked Dicky to excuse her and flew upstairs. Her mother was waiting in the drawing-room, and there followed not only a severe reprimand but chastisement in the form of a sharp slapping.

Her capacity for logic has always been poor. Her approach to most problems was emotional. I say most, because I want to be fair. There have been occasions when she showed that she could be practical. For instance, when my father was out of work, she set to and made pastry which she sent out to various offices and homes by a servant, in a tray, and sold. This she did every day, save Saturdays and Sundays, every week, and it was hard work. I remember those trays of pastry. Also, in later years, it was she who took action and saw to it that I was given a secondary education! My father had wanted me to leave school and look for work when I was fourteen or fifteen, or, at any rate, continue at the primary school until sixteen or seventeen. A crisis brought out the practical in her, but in everyday, run-of-the-mill situations she was hopelessly illogical and ineffectual. Though she would narrate in elaborate detail the tales of my grandmother's severity towards her and her sisters, there would be no resentment in her voice. Nor did she think it necessary to be less severe with her own children. For the slightest misdemeanour my sister and I received a thrashing or a slapping. She kept a small leather thong—a black thing about two feet long—for the special purpose of flogging us when naughty. It was called Tickle Toby.

The older I get the greater grows my contempt for the pontifications of psychologists. People, I am convinced, are born what they are. Environment and "traumatic" experience cannot change character. Put an honest, decent individual in a sewer and he will emerge honest and decent. Under the best of conditions, a neurotic will remain a neurotic. A sane man will still be sane even after he has been made to stand on his head for a year. We are each one of us a mass of inherited contradictions and inconsistencies. There is no set "behaviour pattern". This is my firm belief.

My father had his violent tempers, and often made me shiver and urinate in terror when he shouted at me, but he never once gave me a flogging. Nor did he ever my sister—nor later my two brothers. As I have remarked before, in his rage he would dance in agitation. Shuffle his feet about and clench his hands and shake them at you. But he never struck a blow. My mother, soft and sentimental, tender and considerate to the point of molly-coddling, turned abruptly into a stern chastiser and belaboured us with her hand or that leather thong, her eyes ablaze, her voice as savage as the whacks she delivered.

We had not moved into the Coburg Street place very long

when my father's ordeal came to an end. He was called to the Town Hall and offered a post as an accountant in the Town Clerk's Office. But the salary was very small, so it was decided that it would be best for us to remain where we were for the time being.

Chapter Four

VISITORS AND NEIGHBOURS

TIMES MAY have changed the names of meals in Guiana, but up to when I left there for good in 1941 the first meal of the day was still known as tea, the second meal (mid-day) as breakfast, with lunch at four or five and dinner at seven or eight in the evening. Tea consisted of cocoa or coffee or chocolate—seldom tea—and bread and butter and cheese or an egg. The mid-day meal featured meat or fish and rice and vegetables; the rice was always boiled; never in the form of pudding as it is known in England. Lunch in the afternoon meant a glass of lemonade with biscuits or pastry. Dinner was a heavy meal like the one at mid-day—in fact, like dinner in England or anywhere else in the civilised world.

Breakfast was a magic-word for me in that shadowy era. I associated it always with the lovely lady—I called her Aunt Mary—who hurried in every day at noon to have breakfast with us. Her full name was Mary Fraser—of the Fraser family already referred to—and it appeared that she worked in an office in the Strand, and had evidently arranged with my grandmother to drop in for her mid-day meal at our place during the week. She spoiled me tremendously, for she invariably brought me sweets, and she was very pretty and took me on to her lap and made me feel I was of much importance. She smelt very feminine and perfumed, and her laughter was gay. She was a free and easy creature who made a striking contrast with the stern discipline embodied in my mother and aunts and grandmother. Note that I omit my father. The reason for this is that I cannot remember him exerting much authority over me after our arrival in Coburg Street. Though his attitude towards me remained unchanged, he seemed to have allowed my mother and the other women in the home to assume complete control over us children. He never ordered us about, never corrected us, and, as I have already said, never chastised us. Inherently shy and self-effacing (my mother has often chucklingly related how he used to bolt inside when ladies called at the manse and surprised him reading in the drawing-room), he began to retire more and more into himself. He had a strict routine that began at dawn; he got up every morning without fail at five, Sundays as well as weekdays.

Other entrancing visitors were the Andrew girls. There were two or three of them, and they were all fair-complexioned and deliciously attractive. They lived in the next street, King Street. Sylvia was the one most fond of me, and she took me out for walks sometimes, and once to the cinema. This—I fidget in shame—was a disastrous venture. Some comic feature was being shown, and I yelled in fright when the hero abruptly overturned a table and its contents. Sylvia had to hurry me out and take me home.

Relations with our immediate neighbours were cordial but, somehow, perpetually precarious.

The East Indian family to the west of us had been accepted into middle-class circles, for Mr. Edward Luckhoo was a solicitor—a legal man who, professionally, was on the same footing as that of Mr. Tyrer Egg on our east. But those were the days when only a very few East Indians had "emerged" from the plantation swarm of coolies—a people looked down upon socially by the whites and middle-class admixtures. So even though we were friendly with the Luckhoos—and this continued until I was about fifteen or sixteen—there persisted among my aunts and my mother a continual whispering snobbism. . . . My sister and I were made to feel that we could go over and play with the children, but that it must not be overdone. . . . "After all, they're not really our sort," my mother might murmur. Or my aunt: "Those are people you can't trust. They're so secretive and cunning. Coolies! H'm!"

With the Eggs relations were freer and more relaxed. Old Mother Egg and my grandmother, both blue-eyed and Caucasian, were unquestionably social equals. And Mr. Tyrer Egg, though of mixed blood, was fair-complexioned like my own parents. Mother Egg came over to us, and my grandmother and aunts and mother went over, and the two homes were almost like a joint concern.

Yet, one day, something went wrong—and I was the cause. All I recall is that Mother Egg came over simmering with fury and went into conference with my grandmother. Soon a quarrel was in progress, and the burden of it was that Mother Egg had complained to my grandmother about a remark I made to her when I was alone over there that morning—or it might have been the afternoon before. Mother Egg said that when she had tried to take me into her lap I had said: "No. I mustn't sit in your lap." And when she asked me why not, I had replied: "Mother says I mustn't because you don't like me. Only Lucille you like." And when further pressed by Mother Egg, I had said: "Mother says I'm too dark, and you don't like me to come over here."

How, Mother Egg argued, could the child have said a thing like that to her if he had not really been told it? Why should Rosa have tried to put such an idea into his head? The details of the row are hazy, but I remember that my mother insisted that Mother Egg had been showing a marked preference for my sister because my sister was fair complexioned.

Whether this row had far-reaching effects or not I cannot say, but I know that as the years went by the two families drifted farther and farther apart. It happened gradually, but it happened. Mother Egg died, and when Dicky Egg, a magistrate, with his family, was transferred by the government to another part of the colony we were barely on speaking terms.

On the other hand, relations with the Luckhoos became closer and closer. Whist, parties and dances served as the chief cementing forces.

Before Lucille and I began to go to school, we had only ourselves as company in our play. We were not allowed to mix with any other children of our age—not even the Luckhoo children.

My first introduction to the sphere of lessons was not a pleasant one. I began as the sole pupil of a spinster lady. Miss Eugenie Fraser. Yes, once again the name of that fateful family must be mentioned. She was the elder sister of Aunt Mary, the lovely charming creature who brought me sweets at mid-day when she dropped in for lunch (B.G. breakfast).

Unlike her olive-complexioned younger sister, Aunt Eugenie was a ghostly white, with hair which she plaited and coiled up on top her head in a severe spinsterish bun. In accordance with the fashion of those days, she wore a narrow black velvet band around her throat, and it added to the severity of her appearance, somehow, for it made such a striking contrast with the whiteness of her skin. I used to be fascinated by the pulsing tiny blue veins that seemed to swell and pulse with more rapidity around the black band when she spoke in an impatient voice.

She lived with her brother—Uncle Angus—in a small cottage in the next street—King Street—and she earned her living as a seamstress. All day she sat in the tiny back room, a sort of dining-room-cum-pantry, and snipped-snipped at paper patterns and dress material, or settled down before her sewing-machine which could be heard whirring and whining like a little animal that she was trying to browbeat into subjection.

She would leave me in the portico to study my lesson-book which contained impossible words of four or five letters like "were" and "there" and "when". For me, any word outside of the group "cat-rat-dog" seemed like adult fare. It was wrong to expect me to understand it. Yet, suddenly and ominously, the machine would grow silent, or the snipping end with the clink-clink clatter of scissors being put down, and the thump of Aunt Eugenie's footsteps sounded in the sitting-room. Out she would come, and, her eyes glaring at me through her pince-nez, which magnified them, she would say to me in a spluttering lisp: "Let me hear you say your lesson." (She pronounced it letthon, and there was always an accompanying spray of spittle.)

Tense and dread-filled, I began to spell out the words in the book and pronounce them. "T . . . H . . . E . . ."

"Yeth? What ith T-H-E?"

"The."

"That'th right. Go on. The nexth word."

"D . . . O . . . G . . ."

"Go on. Thpeak up! Thpeak up! What'th D-O-G?"

Wiping the spray off my cheek, I would reply: "Dog," in

an unsure voice, only to receive an impatient pecking tap on the shoulder.

"Why couldn't you have thaid tho if you knew! Don't waytht my time, child. Go on. The nexth word!"

"R . . . U . . . N . . . S."

"Yeth? What ith R-U-N-Eth?" she asked. But I could not tell her.

The silence lengthened. I fidgeted, staring at the open book.

"You know it. Only yethterday you had that word. What ith R-U-N?"

"Run."

"Well, what ith R-U-N-Eth?" she asked. And I murmured: "Run."

My pigtail had recently been cut off or she might have tugged it hard. Instead, she grasped my shoulder and shook me. "How could R-U-N and R-U-N-Eth be the thame thing, child!"

Something congealed in my brain. Fear blocked the synapses.

She dragged me up from the chair and shook me. "What ith R-U-N-Eth, child? You know it. It'th a thimple word you did before!"

"I don't know, Aunt Eugenie!" I blubbered.

"All right. I'll make you know. Come on!" And she began to drag me towards a small empty bedroom on the western side of the cottage the while I struggled and yelled in terror. "No! No! I'll say it, Aunt Eugenie! Don't put me in the room!"

Just on the threshold of the room, she paused and shook me again. "Go on, then! What is R-U-N-Eth?"

I blubbered out something—but it was not the right thing.

She pushed me into the room and pulled the door shut and locked it.

Another terror-scene that is stamped unforgettably on my memory. I can see the rhombuses of sunlight on the dusty floor of that tiny room and live through again at this moment the vacant solitude that seemed to grip me as I stood staring round and shrieking. I felt as though I were locked in that room forever, that I would never again see anyone who cared about me. My parents, my sister and aunts and the servants in

Coburg Street had vanished into the infinite distance that stretched away beyond the silence of the enclosing walls. I hammered on the door with my fists, stamped and shrieked in a mad panicked fright.

This incident occurred more than once. Whenever I couldn't spell out and pronounce a word she locked me in this room. The most harrowing occasion was that on which I failed to recognise T-H-E-R-E.

These sessions lasted from mid-morning to about three in the afternoon. One of the servants took me over to Aunt Eugenie's by what was known as a "cross-cut". This simply involved using the pathway that meandered across the open patch of land between the two streets. It was always a journey of dread. At noon the servant brought my breakfast in a tray covered with a cloth. At three she came to fetch me. Shining, heavenly hour!

If I told a psychiatrist that I suffer from claustrophobia—and I do have an irrational fear of lifts and of being locked into bathrooms and lavatories—he would probably say that these early experiences are what brought to life this state of things. Yet how would he explain the fact that I feel an inordinate sense of safety in a ship's cabin, no matter how tiny it may be? I am never happier and more free from any sensation of dread or panic than when settling down to sleep or moving about in a ship's cabin.

Fortunately, however, my stint with Miss Eugenie Fraser did not last very long. Vaguely I seem to remember some falling out between her and my mother. Perhaps I told my mother of the punishment I received for not knowing my lessons and she tackled Aunt Eugenie on the matter. At any rate, it was decided to send me to my Aunt Louise's private-school.

Chapter Five

GENEVA ACADEMY

"ROSEDALE" was the name of the house in which my aunts lived. It could be justly called a house, for it was fairly large; of two stories and enough rooms to accommodate not only my two official aunts (Louise and Jane) and one unofficial aunt (Carrie) but also, at a later date, my Uncle Bertie and two or three boarders. It was not far from where we lived in Coburg Street. You walked east for about a hundred and fifty yards to the end of the western half of Coburg Street, and turned right into Main Street, and proceeded about fifty yards, and there was "Rosedale" on your right, dead opposite to Westbourne Villa, the three-storied house (with sixty-foot tower) where lived the one dentist in the town and his family.

Geneva Academy was what my Aunt Louise (hereinafter Aunt Lou) called her private school, no doubt in memory of her father's Geneva Academy at the Lutheran Manse. But times had changed somewhat, and this new Geneva Academy, in respect to its social attitudes, had adjusted itself in accordance with the changes. It was exclusive but not quite as exclusive as the nineteenth-century version run by my grandfather. Among its pupils were the three Soares girls—and they were Portuguese. And at that time, Portuguese, like East Indians, had not yet qualified as middle-class. Like the East Indians, they had come to Guiana as immigrants—labourers for the sugar plantations. Though, unlike the East Indians, they had proved bad labourers because of poor physique, but very good door-to-door peddlers of small merchandise, especially textiles. And even better rumshop proprietors and pawnbrokers. Their standards of living were low, because they were thrifty and determined to amass money in as short a time as possible. They dressed carelessly, lived in poor quarters—generally in rooms at the backs of their pawnshops, rumshops or provision shops; many of them were illiterate. And they were Roman Catholics.

It was a "concession" on the part of Aunt Lou that the Soares girls had been admitted into Geneva Academy. No wonder they were regarded as our star pupils. My aunt was always holding them up as the best-behaved and most diligent children in the school, and advising the rest of us to take example.

Among the unruly ones were, apart from myself, the two Glyn-Williams boys, Eric and Gerald, noted for their freckles and fiery red hair, and the two von Ravensburgs—Fritz and Otto. And there was the tall, thin girl with frothy fair hair—Shirley H.—noted for her tears. She was perpetually weeping over something. And my cousins, the Joneses—Harry, Victor and Estelle. My Aunt Elfreda had married a plain Henry Jones. Though I must be careful not to include Harry and Estelle among the unruly ones. They were getting on for ten or eleven, and looked on as "seniors". They were well behaved, and even helped out on occasion, hearing the very young children say their alphabet.

Among the well behaved, too, were the two de Haart girls—Winnie and Rose—and John Davis, the dentist's son from across the street, and his elder sister, Eudora.

In this atmosphere, I began, for the first time, to assert myself. When Shirley H. was scolded by my aunt for some tiny trifle and burst into tears, I was one of those who joined in thumbing noses at her and throwing out "teasing" remarks. The others were Fritz and Otto von Ravensburg and Victor Jones and Eric and Gerald Glyn-Williams. We constituted the Tough Set. Yet there was no *esprit de corps* among us. If one of the group was put to stand in the middle of the room for misconduct the others taunted him. If it was Gerald or Eric in disgrace we bombarded him with comments in reference to red hair or freckles. If Fritz or Otto or myself, the others grimaced and called: "Hun!" . . . "Down with the Kaiser!" . . . "Look at who's standing out there! Von Mittelholzer!"

This kind of conduct was only possible when Aunt Lou was out of the school-room. Often she had to be in the drawing-room to take some casual pupil in piano lessons, or painting or drawing, or the violin. Even the mandolin.

The instant she entered silence fell like a smothering cloak. She was an erect, military woman, with a voice and manner not unlike a sergeant-major's. A stern disciplinarian, she spoke always with a bark, was brisk and precise in her movements, perpetually alert, and always efficient in everything she did.

Aunt Jane (hereinafter Aunt Janie) assisted her in the school, but she was by no means a disciplinarian. Frail, fussy, easily flustered, she spoke in a high, worried whine, and her movements were indeterminate and fumbling. She scolded often, but her words never carried any sting. No one took her seriously. She wagged her finger and threatened, but her wrath was a tinsel one. The gigglings and the babblings continued. Only one thing Aunt Janie had in common with her elder sister—the narrow, black velvet band she wore round her throat. It was a long, white throat not unlike Miss Eugenie Fraser's.

The journey to school in the morning, accompanied by the housemaid or cook, was never one of dread. I am not certain that I learnt much, but the variety of faces and voices interested me, especially the feminine ones. Even at that early age I developed crushes on girls. I remember being attracted especially to Vera Soares who had large dark eyes and a very mischievous smile contained in an oval face surrounded by shifty dark hair. Also, the change of scene—after the sheltered gloom of the Coburg Street place—was stimulating to my imagination, even if somewhat frightening because of the clash of temperaments among us children.

Once, during some childish illness which confined me to bed for a few days, I missed school to such an extent that I insisted on "writing a letter" to Aunt Lou. I was given a pencil and a piece of lined paper, and I filled it with pot-hooks, and my mother and aunts assured me that it would be sent to Aunt Lou. When I turned out to school again, Aunt Lou confirmed that she had received it. Rare event! She smiled and chuckled.

Being a nephew of the schoolmistress put me in a peculiar position. Long after school was shut—at about four or five in the afternoon—my father often brought me and my sister to

"Rosedale", and in the empty school-room—or in the large portico—we would sit and spy at pictures in a stereoscope. Views of the Alps, interiors of famous cathedrals, winter scenes with trees burdened with snow. And while Lucille and I were thus engaged, my father would leave us for a few minutes to go round the corner to buy *mittai* (a Chinese confectionary) from old Mother Chung, a vendor of Chinese sweets and peanuts in St. Ann's Street.

Some afternoons he would vary the routine and take us to the Lutheran Church, and sit with us on the western steps, or, if the sun was too sharp, on the eastern steps, and without fail he would produce from his pocket a brown-paper packet of *mittai* or peanuts contained in a funnel-shaped screw of paper.

A huge sandbox tree stood near the entrance-way to the western lawn. I have been told that in the old days, when the white planters came to church, their slaves had to sit under the shade of this tree and wait. They were forbidden to advance any nearer than this point. The church was no place for slaves.

My sister and I had many a happy frolic on this lawn, watched by my father who sometimes produced some periodical—either *Titbits* or *Pearson's Weekly*—and glanced through it while we played.

Sometimes the nurse would bring us, but inevitably my father would appear on the scene with the routine supply of *mittai* or peanuts. Other nurses with their charges generally preferred to remain on the eastern side of the church, where it was always cool, being in the shadow of the church, but my parents—or most likely my mother—had ordered that we must be kept to ourselves on the western side when the eastern side was thickly populated, using the sandbox tree for shade from the fierce sunshine. This did not please our nurse, who, naturally, liked to fraternise with her colleagues and indulge in a cosy gossip session. But she dared not disobey, especially as my father always turned up to bring us refreshments.

Occasionally, however, the other nurses, on a cloudy afternoon, would establish themselves under the sandbox tree, and then our own nurse was happy, though my sister and I would still keep to ourselves, sitting on the church steps and staring at the gambols of the other children on the lawn, waiting for our father to appear.

For a middle-class father, this behaviour of his was highly unconventional; indeed, utterly eccentric. His appearance never failed to produce a giggling twitter amidst the nurses. Some of them, in a spirit of daring, threw out remarks that could be overheard by my father. But—and I admire him for this—he refused to surrender. Relentlessly, every afternoon, he came marching along, stiff and stolid, his pockets bulging with packets of the crisp sugared fingers of *mittai* and the funnel-screws of peanuts. Chip-chip-tramp across the lawn—sit down on the church steps—crackle of paper and smell of *mittai*—jaws going and the peanut shells beginning to gather in a heap on the step: a heap that would later be carefully transferred back into the brown paper to be taken away and thrown into some dust-bin.

Once or twice—and I do not admire him for this—he would overhear a remark that wounded him in some special way, and he would leave us and hurry over to the nurses and crash out several broadsides of invective at them—nothing obscene, but salvos containing the full pent-up fire-power of his negrophobia. He would stamp and shout and splutter, and even to my five- or six-year-old eyes it was an undignified sight. It embarrassed me and, I am sure, my sister, too. And our own nurse as well.

It was during these church-steps sessions that he was chiefly able to communicate with me and my sister. At home he hardly ever glanced at us. He would stroke our heads and murmur: "Goat-hair." Then with a glance towards the nurses: "Not sheep-wool. They have sheep-wool." And he would stroke his own hair and smile and add: "We have goat-hair." And it might have been on these church-steps—though it could have been in the portico at "Rosedale"—that he told us about his chats with Mr. von Ravensburg, the father of Fritz and Otto; he was pure German but a naturalised British subject, and had even married a creole woman—a near-white. He was connected with some concern called the Consolidated Balata Company (my Aunt Bertha's husband, Bishop Duggin, had a lot to do with it, too). Mr. von Ravensburg and my father met occasionally, it appeared—the family lived in the street next to ours on the southern side, Charlotte Street—and the two of them had chats about the war and about their common German blood. Probably my father must have told him about my grandfather's hero—the great Bismarck—and of his own admiration of the German people. Anyway, my father was fond of telling us about these chats. I can remember once especially when he said with great earnestness: "Mr. von Ravensburg was telling me. He said: 'Just *one* drop of that great blood. Just one drop in your veins, and it makes you different from everyone else. German blood!' "

Yet, there were other occasions when he would express as much horror as my mother or aunts at some account of German brutality in Belgium or France—some atrocity story of women and children being bayoneted in cold blood.

He has never been a great music lover—but he had one passion in this sphere. Military marches. I have seen him, in later years, sit for an hour or longer before the wireless listening to a programme of marches played by a brass band. And he kept his hair cropped short. Every two or three weeks he had it cut. "It's manly to keep your hair short," he has often told me. He never mentioned that Prussian guardsmen favoured this style. Perhaps he knew, or perhaps he did not. My mother would have liked him to grow his hair long, for she has told him: "You have such straight, smooth hair. I can't see why you have to keep it so close." The strong implication here was that only people with "doubtful" (frizzy or very curly) hair had need to crop it close in order to conceal as much as possible the damning negroid cork-screws . . .

He and Aunt Lou were very much alike. She was also very Teutonic in her attitudes, very efficient, a lover of routine and thoroughness in whatever she did. In fact, she was much more Germanic. She bristled with Discipline. She disciplined herself and loved disciplining others, her sisters and boarders as well as her pupils, her nieces and nephews as well as the servants. And—here she was unlike my father—she was no self-effacing, retiring person. She braved everyone, stood up to every situation that presented itself, was active in the church, arranged concerts and cultural evenings, played the violin and mandolin before public gatherings, or accompanied singers on the piano.

"Rosedale", because of Aunt Lou, was the hub of the arts in New Amsterdam. Painting, drawing, stencil-work, embroidery, the piano, the violin, the mandolin. And Geneva Academy.

Chapter Six

MAGIC MOMENTS

DESPITE THE darkness of the rafters and the discipline of my mother and aunts and grandmother, I cannot say I was unhappy as a *young* boy in the Coburg Street place. For one thing, I have never objected to discipline. And even now at fifty-one, I still believe discipline is a good thing—for adults and for children. And especially in these times of namby-pamby psychology. Children need to be spanked, and regimented, if they are to develop into tolerably civilised beings. Many adults need this, too.

The gloom of the rafters, with its spider-webs and concealed denizens, appealed to the romantic in me, as did the Reveille at dawn and the Last Post at night, and the early-morning cackling of hens and crowing of roosters all over the neighbourhood, for in every back-yard there was a fowl-run or a fowl-coop. My grandmother, like my father, an early riser, could be heard in the twilight of six o'clock in the back-yard calling "Chee-chee-chee!" to the fowls and feeding them. The corn rattled on the ground and eager beaks pecked hungrily, to the accompaniment of gurgling sounds from the roosters and satisfied squawks and cluckings from the hens. Sometimes there might be a hammering, and looking out of a window, you would see my grandmother, aproned and wearing a peaked tweed cap, busy repairing a coop or perhaps nailing new laths to the arbour that supported the stephanotis vine. Or she might be watering the kitchen-garden at the back or the flower-beds in the front-yard. Or she might be heard shouting an imperious command to the cook or the housemaid or Francis, the boy who ran errands and helped generally. He and his sister, Dorith, were orphans, the children of some old servant in the employ of my grandmother. They had been adopted by my grandmother and brought up in the servants' rooms in the bottom-house.

My sister and I were not allowed to play in the yard at all times, either because we might get wet in the rain and contract colds or because the sun would give us fever (pet fallacies of my mother). If the weather was very dry, we might be allowed out of doors in the late afternoon—between four and six—provided, of course, that we were not being taken out by the nurse or my father. And on Saturdays, too, during the morning. And we had to wear shoes. Chigoes abounded in the soil—burrowing fleas that liked nothing better than to get established under a toe-nail and reproduce themselves by laying tiny sacs of eggs.

In the early evening, when my sister and I were being prepared for bed, the mellow notes of the Pohlmann piano might suddenly begin to tinkle through the house. A whim had taken my Aunt Bertha to go into the drawing-room and play. Weeks might pass without a sound from the piano. But suddenly it would happen. Later I came to know these pieces. They were stock items, repeated from time to time. I even eventually came to discover their names. *Siciliana*. *The Druid's Prayer*. *The Rosary*. If the whim took her on Sunday she played *Rock of Ages* or some other hymn-tune appropriate to the Sabbath.

The Sabbath Day was something to be reckoned with. No matter how impaired were your senses you simply could not fail to know it was Sunday. The routine of the whole house changed. No baking of pastry or working of sewing-machines. My grandmother's apron and tweed cap vanished. She put on her Sunday clothes, generally black silk, with black hat to match, and went off to church. And there could be no mistaking church-time. The air jangled with the criss-cross tangle of church-bells. From the north came the middle-register belem-belem! of the Presbyterian Church. From the east the hoary, chilly clang-clang! of the Congregational Chapel. From the south the soft, velvety, haughty beng-beng! of the Anglican All Saints parish-church. From the south-west, the high-pitched fire-bell-like Lutheran Church pilling-pilling! And from the same direction, roughly, the Wesleyan Methodist bell competed, though farther away, a kind of dreary metallic wail.

Before the days when my sister and I began to attend the Lutheran Sunday School (it was considered more suitable than the Anglican Sunday School which was run by negro teachers, the pupils also being not suitable companions for us), my grandmother would make us sit in small chairs before her in the dining-room and tell us Bible Tales. This was my first introduction to such stories as the Flood, David and Goliath, Samson and the Philistines, Jezebel. Standard Old Testament fare. She had an illustrated Bible, and showed us the pictures to back up her stories. Here was the army of Pharaoh being engulfed by the Red Sea. Here was Samson pushing apart two giant pillars, and the whole house collapsing around him and people falling in a tangle of arms and legs from the room over his head. Here were the revellers around Belshazzar and the fateful writing appearing on the wall.

My sister and I looked forward to these occasions, for my grandmother was an excellent raconteur. She had a wonderful sense of drama, and used not only her voice but also her hands and face to convey the colour and excitement of any story she told. And she had imagination, and would often digress to tell some little true story of her own experience to illustrate a moral. There were no intermediary shades in her scheme of morality. People were either good or bad, wicked or righteous. A villain was a thorough villain, and his fate was in no doubt: he would end up with Satan and his Black Angels in that terrible place of fire and brimstone called Hell. The hero or heroine would sail up to Heaven to acquire wings and drink milk and honey to the perpetual accompaniment of harp music.

And she made it sound convincing.

So strong were her beliefs, and so confident in manner was she, that she spun about me an atmosphere of security. Nothing, I felt, could possibly go wrong when she was present. The heavenly Guardian Angels she told us of were on her side, and though Satan's Black Angels might be hovering up in the darkness of the rafters, I could fall asleep at night with the complete assurance of protection from Grandma and the Guardian Angels.

Two occasions of glittering excitement brightened those twilight days. The carriage-drive to Cumberland and the arrival of Uncle Bishop.

In those days, and much later, the name Cumberland had no English associations. Cumberland, for me, was a little village on the Canje Creek, three miles from New Amsterdam. Grandfather David Leblanc, as Travelling Postmaster (one rank below Postmaster General), made periodical trips to all parts of the colony to visit the various post-offices. To visit those on the lower Canje Creek he came to New Amsterdam, stayed at a boarding-house, and then dropped in on us, but from what I recall, this drop-in was very brief. In fact, I can only remember the carriage stopping at the gateway and my mother and sister and myself going down and getting in with him, and the coachman flicking his whip and the carriage moving off. I have no memory of my grandmother greeting him or in any way communicating with him. He was always immaculately dressed, with bowler hat and umbrella neatly rolled in English style, and he always spoke in a soft voice and with a pleasant smile. His manner was notable for its calm. He never waved his hands about or revealed any signs of excitability. Such a contrast with the dramatic voice and gestures of my grandmother and the irritable outbursts—or weak, weeping displays—of my mother and aunts!

For me and my sister—and probably for my mother, too—there was a special magic in this morning drive to Cumberland. It was not often we had a carriage-drive, and the countryside seemed like some vast foreign land a long, long way from the antimacassars of Coburg Street.

The advent of Uncle Bishop was an entirely different kind of excitement. No carriage and calm and soft-voiced cultivation. For Uncle Bishop Duggin (why his parents should have named him Bishop baffles me!) was no drawing-room man. A gentleman, yes, or my Aunt Bertha would not have married him, but a gentleman with a he-man manner. Film-star-handsome—he had a small moustache and a "flashing" smile—he arrived with a shout and a bellow of laughter, hugging my aunts and mother and grandmother and slapping my father on the back. And he was always in shirt-sleeves. For he was a bush-man. He led expeditions into the jungle, and was absent for weeks and months at a time, engaged in timber-cutting and balata-bleeding. He travelled in tent-boats, in canoes and on rafts, in launches. A man of romance and adventure who had encounters with snakes and wild animals and Indians, who slept in a hammock slung up between the branches of a tree, who shot game with a double-barrelled gun (my aunt had one safely put away in her room) and risked his life over dangerous rapids and falls.

In the north-western corner of the back-yard stood a star-apple tree, and under its sheltering foliage, on low stands, were to be seen about half a dozen bee-hives. They were Uncle Bishop's, and whenever he came he would spend a lot of time attending to them, and for my sister and me this was the peak-point of his sojourn. Nothing gave us greater pleasure than to watch him in kid gloves and hat and white veil hurrying to and fro between the hives and the bottom-house, a large frame of honeycomb in his grasp. We had to watch from a window, but sometimes the Authorities condescended to let us go downstairs for a short while, especially when he had reached the stage of squeezing the honeycomb and bottling the honey. In the course of this operation, naturally, we always benefited to the extent of at least two or three chunks of honeycomb.

Even when he was absent his presence seemed to linger about the house like wisps of some exotic incense. My aunt might suddenly produce the double-barrelled sixteen-bore shot-gun so that my grandmother could clean it (Grandma was adept at innumerable little jobs, from tree-pruning and coop-repairing to cleaning guns and baking cake), and this would be the occasion for my aunt to relate some incident told to her by Uncle Bishop—an adventure of his in the bush when he had shot a tapir or peccary or a *camoodie* (boa-constrictor). Or the discovery might be made that Uncle Bishop had deposited in some corner a collection of small chunks of balata (the rubbery gum bled from the bullet-tree). Once he left a whip fashioned out of the tough, grey-black substance with its waxy, boot-polish smell. And once a perfectly rounded ball which I immediately wanted to possess. But . . . "What! A balata ball!" exclaimed Mother. "Nothing of the sort! It's too heavy for a child to handle. You'll get into some mischief with it, besides." So I had to resign myself to seeing it put away into the Sacred Drawer with other forbidden articles: Grandma's hammer and chisel and saw, the brown-paper containing the "soft-grease" that was put to several uses, including that of rubbing on the nose of anyone suffering from a heavy cold, discarded bed-castors, full and empty boxes of Rough-on-Rats poison.

Uncle Bishop owned a plantation high up the Canje Creek,[1] which is a tributary of the Berbice River. It was called Don Carlos, and was situated not far from the one-time plantation where the Berbice slave insurrection started in 1763. On this plot of land he grew a variety of crops, and periodically a crate—sometimes two crates—would turn up, sent down by Uncle Bishop on the launch from Don Carlos. In it would be no conventional vegetables like sweet-potatoes, cassavas or yams, but really exciting jungle products—a small sackful of *cookerits* (the fruit of the *cookerit* palm, sweet and oily), another sack containing *awaras* (bright orange and meaty, also from a palm), bullet-fruit from the bullet-tree, *paraipee* seeds from the *paraipee* palm that later would be boiled and eaten with salt at table. And nestling right at the bottom, perhaps, would be a collection of *sawari* nuts looking like fist-shaped rocks the colour of rusty iron; nothing lighter than a large mallet was required to smash their shells, but inside reposed the softest, smoothest and sweetest nut-kernel I have ever tasted.

To the west, right across the grounds of the Luckhoos' place and over on the other side of the Strand, the chief business thoroughfare, there was a saw-mill, run by a big timber company. All day, and sometimes all night, the lulling chug-chug of its engine could be heard as logs of greenheart or *mora* were dragged up from the mud-flats of the river-bank and sawn into boards. In a vague way my child's imagination linked this sound with Uncle Bishop and the jungle, for I had heard that he had to do with timber as well as balata. In fact, it was quite possible that many of the rafts that perpetually arrived at the saw-mill were sent down by him from far up the Creek.

This saw-mill sound was heard and not heard: it never disturbed anyone. It became part of the pattern of sounds in the neighbourhood; the ear had absorbed it into that web of silence composed of tiny, familiar noises: the peep-peep of chickens going to bed, the high-pitched churr of crickets, the

[1] *See* Appendix 2.

tramp of military footsteps over at the police-station and the barking of voices, the chirrup of tree-frogs—especially the tree-frogs in the front garden of the cottage obliquely opposite where lived a spinster called Miss Merriman: a sound that began at six o'clock in the afternoon and continued until six the next morning when daylight broke.

I fell asleep hearing the bugle-calls and the saw-mill's chug-chug, and accepted it as part of my child's life in a house with a high roof and gloomy rafters, part of being in a feather-bed with my long pigtails of "goat-hair", part of the blissful unknowingness and uncaringness of what was happening on the street or in other countries. The Kaiser was a bad man with a big black moustache twirled up in a peculiar way. He had started a big war. But what was that to me? The saw-mill was chugging and the crickets were churring. Miss Merriman's frogs chirruped shrilly—and was that moonlight glittering on the leaves of the guava tree outside the bedroom window? . . . A carriage was going past in Coburg Street. Clip-clop!

Chapter Seven

THE LIGHT—AND THE SNARL

PERHAPS IT IS not the same with everyone—or perhaps it is—but, for myself, when I look back on my childhood my memory of my own identity tends to be swamped by the background scene and the adult figures in it. I see myself as a static dot of light eclipsed by the mobile and authoritative glare of grown-ups. I planned nothing for myself, made no decisions, had no responsibilities, was a passive spectator of the conflicts around me, knew the significance of no event. My mother and aunts quarrelled and wept, but it meant to me only that they seemed unhappy when they were doing this; the cause I could not fathom. I cried when my mother cried, feeling a sense of disaster, but why I should have felt so I could not have explained.

In 1915, the house was completely renovated, two bedrooms being added and a veranda-gallery. Electric lights replaced the oil-lamps. For weeks there was a chaos of carpenters and sawing and hammering and painting. Giant events, with me a pigmy of no importance being fed, dressed, taken to school, brought home and put to bed. Nowadays a barber came to trim my hair. I looked like a boy—a boy with manly goat-hair. No word or gesture of mine could alter the course of the mighty river of achievements.

There were two occasions, however, when the tiny static light that was me glowed brighter and bigger—occasions when something awoke in the pigmy and glared around with an intense awareness.

I must have been about seven, for I was wearing a sailor suit on both occasions. I was photographed in a sailor suit at about that age.

One Sunday afternoon I fell into the large ornamental pond in the Promenade Garden and was drowned.

Well, anyway, that was what the Authorities assumed had happened.

My sister and I were taken by the nurse to the garden for the usual afternoon outing. For some time we sat on a bench and watched the other children and their nurses go by—and the young men and their girl-friends (if young men were allowed to walk out with their girl-friends in those days; I am using my imagination on this point). The garden was always crowded on Sunday afternoons.

Suddenly, and not unnaturally, the nurse suggested that we should go for a walk along the shell-covered pathways that meandered among the trees and shrubs and flower-beds of the garden. Perhaps she felt like meeting one or other of her acquaintances for a gossip. Somehow, I did not like the idea and said that I preferred to sit where I was, so she went off with my sister and was soon lost to sight among the promenaders.

I took off and put down beside me on the bench my sailor-hat—a wide-brimmed thing of straw with a black band bearing the legend: H.M.S. *Renown*; the type of hat worn by naval ratings in Nelson's time.

I sat there, not minding at all being alone, and gazed with dreamy interest at prams and nurses and children. Time passed, and the sun got lower in the west. I began to look around with some anxiety, wondering why the nurse and my sister had not yet returned. But not for long. Suddenly I became aware of voices raised in excitement, and it seemed that people were pointing at me. Then my nurse came hurrying up with my sister. She was in a half-hysterical state.

"Mass'[1] Edgar, where you been to?" she asked.

"I was here," I said, staring at her in wonderment. "What's wrong?"

"We was searching all over de garden for you. Your fadder come and we couldn' find you." Evidently she had forgotten on which bench she had left me. "He gone and tell de police. Somebody find your hat in de pond."

"But my hat is here on the bench . . ."

I was mistaken. When I glanced beside me there was no hat.

"You musta got up and go to de pond, and your hat fall in. We was thinking you must be get drowned."

[1] *See* Appendix 3.

"But I didn't move from the bench here," I said.

"What happen to your hat, den? How it get in de pond?"

"I don't know," I said. "I had it here beside me."

She was not convinced. She insisted that I must have got up and wandered off towards the pond. It never occurred to her that some other child might have snatched up my hat in passing without my noticing and taken it and flung it into the pond (which is what I am convinced must have happened), and I was so bewildered that I myself did not think of putting forward this theory. I simply went on telling her that I had not moved from where I was while she was away.

In the middle of this debate my father came hurrying up, my sailor-hat, dripping wet, in his hand. He seemed frantic but relieved to note that I had been found undrowned. He began to gesticulate and shout at me, asking me why I had got up and wandered off to the pond. Think of the anxiety I had caused everyone!

Baffled, I repeated my story. I had not left the bench for a single moment while the nurse was away.

But he would not believe me.

I was hauled off home, and my mother, who, it appeared, had already heard the rumour that I had been drowned, was also in a state of agitation. But relief at seeing me did not prevent her from putting me through the same third-degree that the nurse and my father had inflicted on me. Hadn't I been warned over and over that I must never approach anywhere near that pond?

In tears, I stuck to my story. I had *never* moved. *Never*. I had sat where I was on the bench all the time.

"Telling fibs into the bargain, too, are you? Very well. I'll teach you to tell fibs."

And a savage walloping.

It was during this walloping that something awoke in me. A white, glaring awareness. The utter injustice of what was being done to me, the withering unfairness, crashed into my consciousness like a hurricane. For the first time I felt like hitting back at my mother, snarling and fighting like a tiger. I did fight and scream, but my mother thought nothing of this. Only I within me knew there was more in my display than the usual childish fright and pain concomitant with chastisement.

Something clicked in me. Something angry and adult, something fiery and unforgettable. I knew I was a person, and a person who had been gravely wronged.

The other occasion did not feature so much violence, but it moved me just as deeply. It switched on the light, awoke the Snarl.

It was a photographic occasion. My mother was determined that her sailor-suited son should not be allowed to outgrow his sailor-suit without a pictorial record being made for the future. So she arranged with Mr. Gomes, the Portuguese photographer, who lived in the next street, to the north of us —King Street. Not two doors from Miss Eugenie Fraser. One of the rooms in his little cottage was the Studio—place of the tripod and camera and the black cloth that covered the camera. Place of the wall with the black-and-white backdrop depicting a balustrade and pillars in the classical manner or ornamental iron railings and urn-on-plinth. Place of the little birdie—"Look here! Just here! You'll see a little birdie fly out! Don't move! Just look!" I was familiar with it all, so it would be no novelty when I was taken across in the afternoon.

With great care my mother dressed me for the appointment. How it happened I cannot recall, but perhaps one of my aunts suggested that a dark-blue tie of my father's might go better with my sailor-collar than the puffy silk cravat-cum-bow monstrosity that my mother had invented. Anyway, my mother tried the tie idea, and when I saw myself in the wardrobe looking-glass I smiled my approval. This was it! I felt daring and sailorly. I felt I was about to embark on a dashing escapade aboard a dreadnought—or a cruiser. I not only looked like a sailor but I was wearing a man's tie. I felt like strutting around and throwing out my chest.

Hardly had the mood come upon me, however, when my mother, for some mysterious feminine reason, decided that the tie would not do. She surveyed me and shook her head. No, no. It would have to be the bow, after all. She called it a "bow". The bow would look nicer. I objected. I *wanted* the tie. I *preferred* the tie. I wouldn't look like a sailor if I wore the bow.

"You will wear the bow, I say!"

"No. I don't want the bow. I want the tie!"

"I'm not going to argue with you. You're a child."

I pressed my hand against the tie and resisted her when she tried to take it off. My hand was slapped away. The Authorities were in action. The tie was taken off. But I would not give in. I stamped and yelled.

"I want the tie! I don't want to wear the bow!"

But the tie was put aside and the bow was pinned on.

The Light. And the Snarl. I tore it off and flung it from me.

"I won't wear it! I won't wear it!" I raged. And stamped again. My cheeks glistened with tears of fury. Something had probed and hurt the masculine pride in me. It roused the Me that slumbered in the regimented pigmy. I was ready to mobilise and fight to the end.

But the Authorities were strong—as always. I was slapped, and the bow was put on again. I raged on. And outwardly I surrendered. I let it remain. But within I was still at war. The Battle Light still burned bright. The Snarl rumbled on deep inside.

Eventually I was hauled off to the photographer's.

I went, panting with the conflict that still scalded my being. At Mr. Gomes's studio, I refused to co-operate. The fat, pleasant Portuguese gentleman coaxed, crooned, whispered, promised me sweets—but I refused to smile. Refused to take the scowl off my face.

"Don't you want to see a little blue birdie fly out of here?" asked Mr. Gomes, pointing at his camera covered with a black cloth.

I didn't. And went on scowling.

So he had to take me as I was, with mouth set, with thunder on my brows.

Chapter Eight

SOUNDS AND SWEET AIRS

THE SONG I remember with most nostalgia is *Daisy, Daisy, give me your answer true.* For it was the song associated with my first notable infatuation. I have remarked before that I had a tendency to develop crushes on girls, and that at Geneva Academy I was attracted to Vera Soares. But that and similar crushes were mild in comparison with the crush I developed for Gwen R. She was the daughter of an executive of S.D. & Co., if executive is not the wrong word. However, he was a Chief Something in the firm, and his daughter, my own age, but for a few months, attended Geneva Academy. That is where I first met her. But she also went to play with the Luckhoo children, and now that my sister and I were allowed to go over more often to the Luckhoos, I ran into her there, too, sometimes.

My aunt gave end-of-term school concerts, and I remember myself sitting crouched up in an armchair watching with love-haunted eyes the rehearsals being conducted in the sitting-room. Gwen was one of a line of girls who had to do a sort of English country-dance while they sang *Daisy, Daisy,* Estelle Jones, my cousin, accompanying on the piano and Aunt Lou conducting, hands waving, head nodding to the rhythm of the tune, and every now and then voice barking an interruption. But for me, in my armchair, only Gwen and the tune existed, and both had become welded into one heart-aching symbol of beauty and bliss.

Other music from this period that, if heard now, rings an evocative bell in me is the music associated with the First World War. *Dolly Gray, Tipperary, Johnny, get your gun.* Living right opposite to the central police station as we did gave us the opportunity to witness all the great military occasions. I watched the men who were to form part of the Overseas Contingent gather in the police compound, and saw them march away headed by a military band playing *Tipperary*. And periodically some military unit of one sort or the other—either of the local militia or of civilians being trained for service overseas—mustered on the police parade ground, and inevitably the sound of a deep bass-drum and brass music would crash forth in some blood-tingling march-tune. Or we might hear voices across the way singing one of the popular war-songs.

There was, however, a more irksome side to music. It had to do with Hemy's Tutor. This bright-orange-covered folio-size book began to become a bogey of boredom in my life. My Aunt Bertha had undertaken to teach me to play the piano (she was already teaching Edward Luckhoo, about a year my junior). Every morning after tea (breakfast) I was expected to seat myself before the Pohlmann upright piano, open the Hemy's Tutor on the stand provided, and go through two or three pages of five-finger exercises, and these done, continue to the pages that treated of a series of snippets of well-known "airs"—*Annie Laurie*, *The Blue-bells of Scotland*, *The Loreley*, *La donna e mobile*. I made innumerable mistakes, because I hated the dreary monotony of it—and, of course, the Authorities, in the form of my aunt as well as my mother, came down heavily on me, accusing me of being without ambition. See how well Edward Luckhoo was getting on? *He* had ambition. Why couldn't I be like him?

There were two cinemas in the town—Mr. Barbour's and Mr. Isaacson's. Mr. Isaacson's was called the Olympic, and Mr. Barbour's had a name, too, but it evades me. It probably evaded many people even at that time, too. The reason is that Mr. Barbour was a man of bubbling personality—in another environment he might have become a very successful impresario, even another C. B. Cochran or Bertram Mills—and his personality had overshadowed the name of his cinema. Nobody remembered the name of the concern he ran—only that it was Mr. Barbour's. My sister and I were sometimes taken to matinee shows at his cinema (called a theatre, by the way, not a picture-house or a cinema), and though the films, comics suitable for children, amused me, it was the music that caught my imagination. The piano and violin that accompanied these silent films clanged and wheezed out a continuous cavalcade of waltzes and sentimental airs, and these built up in my fancy pictures of their own that had nothing to do with the films being shown. Dreamy soap-bubble landscapes painted in soap-bubble colours that drifted and burst almost as soon as they came into being but which left indelible perfumed stains on my memory.

Mr. Barbour's cinema was near the Town Hall, about a quarter of a mile along the Strand, from the corner of Coburg Street, but the Olympic was right next to the saw-mill already referred to. Both Mr. Barbour and Mr. Isaacson were friends of the family, and there was a friendly rivalry between them to inveigle my mother and aunts into attending shows. And both were handsome and charming men. Often Mr. Barbour dropped in and by sheer persuasive effervescence got my mother and aunts to agree to go and see a show . . . "I'm *asking* you to come, Rosa. Bertha, I'm *asking* you. I'm inviting you. You're my guests. I *want* you to see this picture. You must see it. You just *can't* miss it." Mr. Isaacson was not quite as effusive as this, but he, too, often succeeded. His speciality was the exciting serial. *The Exploits of Elaine* was one whose title stays in my memory, because my mother and aunts discussed it so much.

The music of the Olympic drifted out and came clearly on the air to me in bed. I fell asleep hearing it—and the chug-chug of the saw-mill. A gentle gust of wind might cause the foliage of the guava tree to rustle, and an owl—a jumbie-bird, the servants called it—might utter a mysterious too-too-toot!, but these were minor interruptions in the night's set programme of perfumed sounds from the Strand . . .

Chug-a-chug . . . Chug-a-chug . . . *The Destiny Waltz* merging into *The Blue Danube* merging into *The Merry Widow* merging into *The Druid's Prayer* merging into *Beautiful Dreamer* . . . From the audience a sudden wailing . . . The villains were after Pearl White. She was in great peril . . . *The Destiny Waltz* . . .

It was about this time that I developed a great passion for time-pieces. Both watches and clocks fascinated me. Many nights I would purposely keep awake just to listen to the teck-tock of the pendulum-clock in the dining-room, clearly audible in the silence of the house, and wait to hear it strike the hours. And later I went one better than this, and formed the habit of creeping stealthily out of bed to go and station myself at the window so that I could listen for the striking of the church clocks. The Anglican and Presbyterian churches both had clocks that struck not only the hours but chimed at the quarter- and half-hours. This seemed to me a precious adventure. No one knew about it. It was a secret between me and me. What would the Authorities have said if it had become known that I stayed up until after midnight at the window to indulge in this absurd occupation! It would have been useless trying to explain to them the terrific thrill I got out of hearing the forbidden hours of eleven and twelve—actually *midnight*!—being struck in the still night-air, and the equally wonderful thrill of *waiting* to hear the next chime.

Very soon, however, I was to grow accustomed to another kind of music. A lonely music. The whistling and moaning of wind through crevices.

Chapter Nine

UMBRELLA BOY

AUNT LOU was very upset. Harry and Victor and Estelle, my cousins, had been educated at Geneva Academy until they were thirteen or fourteen. Why should Mother feel that my sister and I were not progressing? Why should we be removed to other schools?

As usual, my father was indifferent in the matter. But Mother had her way. As a girl, she had been educated at the Roman Catholic convent-school, the only school, it appeared, in the town where the daughters of gentlemen could receive proper tuition in deportment as well as a tolerable education in the essential book-subjects. My mother, therefore, found it no difficulty to arrange for my sister to be accepted as a pupil at the Ursuline Convent School. For me a private-school run by a gentleman called Mr. P. A. Cummings was found. It was an unconventionally run school in that it consisted simply of an annex to the free school maintained jointly by the Government and the Presbyterian Church. Mr. Cummings was the headteacher of this general school attended by the sons and daughters of every carpenter, cook, policeman and tin-smith in the town, but as a side-line he kept this little private-school for the sons of the middle-class (daughters, too) exclusively.

If anyone, say in England or Australia, having reached as far as this chapter, imagines that he has begun, at last, to get into proper focus the pattern of the social scene in British Guiana, let him think again.

Mr. Percival Augustus Cummings was a pure-blooded negro who had married a lady much, much lighter than him-self in complexion. He was a well-bred man—a staunch Presbyterian and a member of the Foresters' Lodge. No one in the middle-class of admixtures questioned his right to be called a gentleman. Apart from the advantage of his marriage, he had an air of ease, and his speech was the speech of a man of the middle-class. In fact, so completely had he been accepted by the middle-class that it was not until I got much older that I thought of him as being a negro. As a boy, I simply regarded him as my teacher, a man sure of himself, a disciplinarian, and a member of the body of adults that pushed around pigmies like myself. In short, like my mother and aunts, he represented the Authorities.

In his private-school there were no negroes. His was the only dark-brown complexion present when he came in to supervise us. He divided his time between the main school and the annex where his twenty or thirty private pupils were accommodated. Occasionally a young teacher, a negress called Miss Knight, would assist him. A very pleasant spinster to whom we all took a liking and for whom I still have a very soft spot.

My experiences during this period were bitter-sweet. So bitter-sweet they could have soured me permanently. And that is not merely an attempt at cheap wit. There is more literal truth in it for me than anyone might imagine. Had I not been born as I was, resilient and trauma-proof, as I believe the majority of us are born (I still thumb my nose at the psychiatrists!), I would almost certainly have grown up to hate my mother, and would, no doubt, have developed all the concomitant complexes, neuroses and psychoses.

At noon, all the pupils of Mr. Cummings's private-school and of the free school were tough enough to go home for their lunch—all except Edgar Mittelholzer who was considered by his mother so delicate that the sun would have given him fever—or the rain pneumonia. No doctor had ever pronounced me delicate. In fact, I kept perfect health. But Mother ruled that precautions must be taken. So I had to remain at school during the lunch-break—the only child in the building. The only human being. I had to sit down or wander around in the wind-humming silence and wait for the servant to come with her tray. She had to walk with my lunch all the way from home—well over a quarter of a mile—and sit and wait until I ate it. Then she left, and once again I had to sit or stand or walk around, listening to the trade-wind whistling and moaning through the open crevices of the wall in the annex where the private school was held. It was a tropical building. The temperature in British Guiana never *falls* below seventy-three, so walls could be thin and wooden, and could even have crevices through which you could see the sky. They are not supposed to have crevices, of course, but it just happened that this annex was in that condition.

Sometimes I liked it. It appealed to my imagination. The emptiness of the building, the looming white church on the south in its grounds green with grass and trees and grey-white with tombstones—very old tombstones. All churchyards in British Guiana do not contain tombstones. Only in the early and middle nineteenth century was it considered all right to bury corpses in churchyards. Later it became unhygienic. The by-laws forbade it. I liked to think of the people buried under these tombstones, tried to imagine what they must have been like in their lifetimes. And the moaning and the whistling of the wind satisfied something poetic in me. On the north of the school was the wide parade-ground where on the King's Birthday and such occasions the local militia and the police held military displays—trooping the colours and so forth—and the wind came unhindered across this expanse of green. Came from where, on the other side of the parade-ground, in a spreading cottage, lived the A—— family. Stella A—— and Stephen A—— were pupils of Mr. Cummings's, and I had fallen in love with Stella. Another Notable Infatuation.

And Stella, like many of the other children, laughed at me and called me a softy because I was not allowed to go home for lunch. Bitter, indeed, scaldingly acid, humiliation. But there was worse.

In the afternoon, just before school broke up, the servant-girl arrived with a large black umbrella. She stood waiting for me at the entrance-way, and as we all trooped out she stopped me, opened the umbrella and held my hand so that I had to walk beside her and be sheltered from the fever-giving rays of the hot afternoon sun.

I don't need to go into much detail in respect to what reactions this performance brought into being among the other children. For me it was the Final Humiliation. At first, I protested fiercely. With the hoots and jeers bombarding me from every point of the compass, I told the servant I would not walk under the umbrella. I told her to close it. But she said that she had been ordered to open it over me. What would the mistress say if she disobeyed? She would lose her job. I made several scenes, and on one occasion she surrendered, and we walked home with furled umbrella. But my mother, generally on the look-out for me, saw us coming, and no sooner had we arrived when she opened fire. The servant explained, I explained—the children laughed at me; I wouldn't have an umbrella; no other children used umbrellas—but it availed naught. The servant was severely reprimanded. I received a flogging, with Tickle Toby, from my mother.

The Battle Light burned bright in my eyes. The Snarl rumbled in me.

But the Authorities won again. I had to submit to the humiliation every afternoon. And every afternoon I was jeered at . . . "Mother's Baby-boy!" . . . "Lump of sugar!" . . . "The sun will melt him!" . . . "Umbrella-boy!"

Yet, during the day, I forgot the agony of the afternoon, and threw myself into all the fun of the few in Mr. Cummings's private-school. I fancied myself as a comedian. The Charlie Chaplin films were very popular at the time, and I aped Charlie Chaplin and got quite a few laughs—even from Miss Knight. In fact, I became a nuisance to her, and once or twice she had to report me to Mr. Cummings. I got several whackings from him—he carried his cane around with him all day—and I deserved every one. I bore them with tearless fortitude, as every boy who was caned did. It was a matter of masculine pride not to cry.

Soldiers came home from the War. There were celebrations. The town was decorated. The Prince of Wales visited British Guiana, and my father was given the commission of executing an illuminated address to be presented to him. Schools all over the town and countryside held processions, and buns and rusks were eaten at treats given in schoolrooms. But young Edgar did not march in these processions, nor did he eat any buns or rusks. Too delicate a boy for such rough-and-tumble goings-on. He had to remain at home and listen to the noises of festivity in the near and far distance.

Not that it bothered me very much that I could not be one of these gatherings. Processions and parties have never appealed to me. I was born with an unsociable streak. I have always liked quiet places, company but not in excess, and the minimum of gaiety. Yet, being left out of these functions gave me a vague sense of inadequacy. No boy likes to be made to feel that he cannot participate in what other boys are participating. In fact, there was a kind of see-saw uncertainty in me. Like my father, I was extremely shy, despite my clowning before my school-mates, and this shyness made me want to be alone. Yet I felt I ought to be allowed to dare the dangers of crowds and the rain and sun from which I was so assiduously protected.

I remember a party at the home of the A—— family. They had moved to a two-storied place at the corner of King Street and the Strand (or it is possible that at this period they had been living here and only later moved to the cottage near the parade-ground). It was supposed to be a birthday party—Stephen's. My sister and I were taken by the nurse and deposited among a roomful of noisy, boisterous children *and* grown-ups, and there was music and dancing in addition to the usual parlour games. Even though I had been thrilled at the idea of attending this party, because I would be near to Stella, and might even be able to dance with her, I was miserable throughout the whole afternoon and early evening, and kept wishing desperately to be taken home. Nor were my reactions any different at another party given by the C—— family (their father was a doctor) at their home in the grounds of the Mental Hospital. Dr. C—— was on the medical staff there. The noise and gaiety disturbed me; I wanted to get away from it. Yet I would have been disastrously disappointed if I had not been allowed to go.

Social occasions I enjoyed were the evenings when Ivy and Maud C—— and their mother, a seamstress friend of my mother's, came on a visit. For on these occasions my sister and I were allowed to stay up an hour or two later than was customary, and Ivy and Maud, about fifteen and sixteen in age, would take us away from the grown-ups and tell us stories. Generally true-life stories about murders and robberies and people who had suffered disasters of one sort or another. They told these stories with an air of grown-up mystery which my sister and I found very impressive. It added to the excitement of the stories. Sometimes the stories were of ghosts and haunted houses, and these were the most thrilling of all.

Other interesting evenings were those when the Frasers came. These were perhaps very distantly related to the Fateful Frasers, if there was any relation at all. They were friends of my grandmother's. Mrs. Fraser, a widow, and Freddie, Muriel and Evelyn. Freddie was about three or four years older than myself, but Muriel and Evelyn were about my age. Often the five of us—the three children, my sister and I—would embark on the unheard-of adventure of exploring the bottom-house and the yard *by dark*! While the grown-ups were engrossed in conversation upstairs in the gallery-veranda (or simply gallery, as we called it), we five would creep away and out of the house, led by the daring Freddie, and go hunting wild animals near the servants' rooms and under the guava and shaddock trees. On moonlight nights there was an added thrill—at least, for me. I have always carried with me a picture of moonlight glittering on the leaves of the trees during one of these expeditions, and I can still smell the strong, sweet perfume of a jasmine bush or the stephanotis on its arbour on the eastern side of the house. We had to speak in whispers, or in very low murmurs, our ears constantly on the alert for a shout from upstairs.

Then there was Olga C—— who came to spend the day sometimes. She was a few months older than I, and was far more interested in my company than my sister's. I don't recall how we engineered it, but somehow we often arranged to be alone together at the end of the gallery, and here the conversation between us inevitably led to the topic of husbands and wives and how babies were born. It was Olga who disillusioned me about the North Pole myth. According to what my aunts had told my sister and me when our brothers were born—Mervyn in November, 1916, and Arthur in September, 1918—babies came from the North Pole, though you had to send to England to order them. The mail-steamer brought them. I accepted this explanation until Olga gave me her own ideas on the matter. She warned me that it was a Dark Secret.

Only grown-ups were supposed to know about such things. I must never, never say anything about it. Did I promise?

I promised. And reassured, she suggested that when she and I grew up we could become husband and wife and have babies of our own.

I agreed enthusiastically.

Chapter Ten

FADING MAGIC

AS LIFE moved on, old magic-moments faded like dead stars and new ones twinkled alive. No longer did Grandfather Leblanc come to take my mother and sister and me to Cumberland in a carriage. He had retired as Acting Postmaster General, doing so, I later discovered, in disgust because if he had remained in the service he would have been compelled to revert back to his previous post as Travelling Postmaster and show the ropes to the Englishman who had been appointed as Postmaster General; in those days it was not considered the correct thing that a fully-fledged Postmaster General should have an olive complexion!

No longer did Uncle Bishop arrive with he-man bellowings of laughter to look after his bees and give us honeycombs. News came that he had died of some bush-sickness. Rumours of all kinds buzzed like nasty flies in the air. One was that he had had a mistress—an Indian girl called Ruby—and that she had poisoned him. Another that the men under him had had a grudge against him and had murdered him. Another that he had contracted black-water fever. Another hinted that he might have been the victim of necromancy.

Meanwhile, Grandma had had a misfortune which resulted in the loss of a leg. Very friendly with all sorts of people, especially church cronies, she had thought it her duty to visit the house of a family called the Hahnfelds, who lived in the eastern half of Coburg Street, early in the morning and on an empty stomach. The night before Mr. Hahnfeld had died of something that involved gangrene, and my grandmother, as a good friend, had to assist in washing the corpse. Very shortly afterwards, it seemed, she developed symptoms of blood-poisoning in one leg. The leg became septic and she had to be rushed to Georgetown to have the leg amputated (the local hospital evidently was not considered good enough for such an operation). I was allowed to be one of the party that accompanied her to the City. New magic! Not only the sixty-mile journey in the Model T-Ford car but Georgetown—a city. Not a mere town but a network of streets and trees and canals of, to me, bewildering complexity. A lovely mirage had taken shape in my fancy. Thereafter every time the name Georgetown was mentioned a magic-bell rang within me. Back in New Amsterdam, my dream was to take a trip to Georgetown. Several trips. Even to live there.

On this first visit, I stayed at the home of some old friends of my Aunt Bertha's—the Cendrecourts—in Broad Street. They were of French descent and very devout Roman Catholics, and there were two brothers, Robert and Henri, and a sister, Josephine. All three of them were pharmacists and kept a shop (called a drug-store, as in the U.S.) on the ground-floor of their two-storied place. The smell of the drugs, like some rare incense in my senses, and the sight of the shelves with their bottles labelled in Latin, became incorporated in my Georgetown myth as strongly as did the waves, grey and muddy, that foamed and roared on the flat beach beyond the Sea Wall, the dyke built to keep out the sea from a lower-than-sea-level city, and the tram-cars that rumbled and clanged along the main streets, including Broad Street, and the canals, and the military band that played in the Botanical Garden and on the Sea Wall promenade.

Among the best magic-moments were those spent over at the Luckhoos. As I have mentioned before, my mother was always reluctant to let us go and play with the Luckhoo children—and this not simply because of any feeling that they were socially inferior. She would say: "You must not be low-minded. If you go over there too often they will fancy you don't care for your own home." She forbade us to go unless we were invited, though the Luckhoos had given us carte blanche and would not have minded if we had gone over every day to play with the children. However, my sister and I had to abide by the ruling laid down by my mother, and we explained to the children why we could not come over every day after school as we would have liked to do. So Mrs.

Luckhoo had to issue formal invitations for my sister and me to spend a Saturday or any other week-day during holiday time. When Edward came for his music lesson he might bring the verbal invitation, or once or twice Lionel, his younger brother, would come to the fence with the message. A day spent with the Luckhoos was always an idyllic one. We played marbles (which we called taws), and there were two games, which, I believe, are Indian, that I was taught to play. One was *airee-doree* (my spelling is phonetic), and was played with two sticks, and another *tagga* played with a circular piece of lead and buttons; the idea in this latter was to throw the piece of lead at a hole in the ground, doing it so skilfully that it should not overlap the line drawn around the hole. If it covered any of the buttons scattered around the hole these buttons were considered "won" and collected by the thrower. Apart from these games, there was the food to look forward to—Indian food done in the real Indian way that was unknown in our own home: hot, strong curries and *roti* and other dishes the names of which I never discovered.

We had no car, but the Luckhoos had one, and there were occasions—the most dazzling of all—when we were invited to spend a day on the Corentyne Coast at the home of some relative or friend of the Luckhoos. But for these trips to the flat, savannah lands of the Corentyne Coast, with their canals and smells and scattered sugar plantations and villages, I would probably never have been able to write my first published novel, *Corentyne Thunder*. It was on these outings that I absorbed the atmosphere of the district and even got to cultivate a deep affection for it.

Meanwhile, despite the prohibitions inflicted on my sister and myself, my mother and aunts cultivated a very close friendship with Mrs. Luckhoo and her sister, Mrs. Phoebe Madhoo, and hardly a day passed without an exchange of visits for whist. Edward and Lionel had soon learnt to play, and would sometimes be called upon to make up a four. Eventually I myself became an expert, and once I was allowed to take part in a whist-drive in aid of some charity, as were also Edward and Lionel.

One might well ask at this point: But what of your father? What part did he take in these social goings-on? The answer is that he took no part in anything. He kept to himself. His routine was to wake at five every morning, have a bath, dress and settle down in a chair with *Pearson's Weekly* to which he had been a regular subscriber since his bachelor days (he had even once been the winner of a competition for overseas readers!) At seven he had his breakfast and then left for the Town Hall. He was not supposed to be in office until nine, but he arrived at eight or before, long before even the most junior clerk, and settled down to work. He came home for lunch at noon, read the newspaper (which arrived by the mid-day train from Georgetown), then returned to work. He arrived back home at about half past four, went for a walk, and eventually found himself in the Promenade Garden where the nurse had taken my two brothers for their afternoon outing.

Just as he had done with my sister and myself, he would take them nuts or sweets, and accompany them home. Then dinner, followed by the ritual of seeing the two boys to bed. My mother or the nurse generally undressed them and put them into bed, but he had to go in and stand by the foot of the bed to hear them say their prayers. This over, he would bustle back into his room, bustle out again with his drawing-paper and pencils and paint-box and sit at the dining-table for a bout of work on some illuminated address that he had been commissioned to do for some departing or arriving Governor or important official, or if no such work was on hand, he would read *Pearson's Weekly*. Then back into his room, and a rustling and bustling as he put away his drawing things or periodical—and then a tinkling sound. He was mixing himself a glass of lemonade. This was his bedtime drink. The sharp scent of the freshly cut lemon would permeate the whole dining-room and the tinkling might go on for nearly a quarter of an hour, for he often added lumps of ice to the drink, and drank it slowly, clinking the ice meditatively as he did so. He was a non-smoker, so no smell of tobacco smoke followed this drink. The last thing he did was to switch off the dining-room light after everyone else had retired.

Round about September, every year, he would be heard grunting and murmuring to himself: "Well, I must be thinking of an idea for a story." For every Christmas he contributed a short-story to the *Christmas Tide*—a magazine published annually by *The Daily Argosy* of Georgetown. He wrote under the initials W.A.M. and the story was invariably about a situation that involved some ironical twist of events in the lives of a middle-aged couple. It was written in a scholarly, rather sonorous style, besprinkled with Latin words or phrases. The prevailing tone was wry; he eschewed sentimentality.

For me, in contrast with the pleasant hours spent playing marbles and other games with the Luckhoos, there was the irksome ordeal I had to endure about twice a week at the home of Mr. Cummings. P.A., as most of us called him, behind his back, somehow appeared to feel that I might have the ability to win a Government scholarship which would entitle me to attend a secondary school at the Government's expense. Why he should have felt so I can't imagine, for I can't recall ever having displayed any brilliance at my school-work. Drawing was the only subject that gave me no trouble, but this was a family disease I had inherited; nothing to exclaim over. However, there it was; he began to concentrate on me and two or three other pupils in his private-school as well as others in the free school. The great incentive, so far as he himself was concerned, was that for every pupil under him who succeeded in getting a scholarship he was awarded a bonus of twenty-five dollars. My arithmetic seemed my weakest point, so he decided to give me extra lessons at his home.

I detested these sessions. I had to sit in his back gallery and frown and wriggle over the problems he set me while he was upstairs pottering about at some domestic task. In the back-yard, his children would be playing—or in the next yard, which was the dentist's, a rough-and-ready cricket match might be in progress—and all these distracting sounds would reach me while I stared around the gallery at the staid Victorian pictures in their heavy frames, and tried to make out the script in some huge framed certificate relating to the Foresters' Lodge. Then the sudden start as P.A. hurried in to supervise what I had done. And always it was the same. I had failed to get out the problem. So he would bend over me and patiently try to explain it. The great trouble was that he believed in formulae as opposed to straightforward reasoning, and I simply could not remember formulae.

I was the least surprised when the results of the examination were published and it was learnt that I had failed to secure a scholarship.

Chapter Eleven

DOCTOR WANG FU

MY FAILURE to win a scholarship might have been the reason, or my mother might simply have felt that some sort of change was necessary. However I was taken from P.A.'s school and sent to another which had recently been founded by a Mr. Adams in a building in Lutheran Court—a building not thirty yards from the house in which I was born.

The novelty of going to a new school appealed to me, but the bitter umbrella situation remained unaltered. Mother refused to be persuaded into feeling that I would survive the perils of the weather as the other boys did protected only by the clothes I wore. Nor would she yield on the question of lunch which the servant brought every day in a tray, as at the other school. This was not a mixed school, and the boys, who had already heard of me as a softy, were savage in their jeers. But I was prepared, and stood up to them. Before long, despite umbrella and servant-fetched lunch, I had won several of them over, and made close chums of at least three. I had begun to collect stamps, and it was this that chiefly fostered the friendships.

Mr. Adams, notwithstanding an unfortunate skin blemish that gave his face a piebald appearance, was popular in middle-class circles. He was an excellent tennis player. He believed in games for his boys, and in the afternoon, after lessons, the senior boys played soccer. It was no regret to me that I was a junior and could not participate, though I liked soccer. Later in my school career it even bloomed into one of my leading passions.

It was at Mr. Adams's school that I became Doctor Wang Fu, head of a mysterious criminal secret society. The silent film serials I went to see at the matinee shows from six to eight featured exciting characters like Doctor Wang Fu, and at school many of us identified ourselves with them. Hence I became Doctor Wang Fu, and Darcy Wishart, one of my chums, was my chief henchman. We were supposed to have in our possession a valuable sheep-skin map that showed where a cache of jewels was buried, and another gang was forever plotting to get it away from us, but we were, naturally, always too clever for them. This kind of make-believe gave us a lot of fun, and added to the excitement and interest of the serials we went to see. The cinema was right opposite to the school in Main Street, and the highly coloured posters were always in view. (Mr. Barbour had by now gone out of business.) Darcy and I kept up this fantasy for a long time. We even found a hiding-place for the square of brown paper that we called the sheepskin, and defied our enemies to discover it.

I did not remain long at this school. Somehow, the diagnosis was made that I was not progressing, and after some discussion it was decided to send me back to P.A. But instead of re-entering the private-school I was put into the free school. I have an idea that my mother had come to the sad conclusion that private-schools were doing me no good from an educational point of view. This was a desperate measure. At all costs the dunce must be yanked out of his rut of sloth and stupidity.

Not that it made much difference. Doctor Wang Fu, now established among a class of black boys, proceeded to indoctrinate a new gang. This time it was not a sheepskin but "crystals". A collection of valuable crystals, each of which held a mysterious secret, had come into the possession of the master-criminal, and the enemies of his secret society were determined to wrest these crystals away for their own gain. Doctor Wang Fu chose a "right-hand man" in the person of Conrad Edinboro, a boy whose father worked at the post-office. He also pointed out certain other boys who, he told his gang, were his enemies. "You keep your eye on them. They're going to try to get hold of the Crystals. We must resist them with everything we've got!" With a sinister laugh. "But no fear! Doctor Wang Fu is too astute. He'll outwit their every move." Sometimes Conrad would come to me and whisper that he had seen suspicious movements in the Promenade Garden—just across the way to the west—and that he believed the other gang was preparing to strike. So Doctor Wang Fu would scribble a hasty message and give it to Conrad to take to our scouts posted at various mythical points in the garden.

The Authorities soon came to hear of Doctor Wang Fu, and threatened that if I did not stop all this nonsense and concentrate on my lessons I would not be allowed to go to the cinema. "What's going to become of you if you don't have an education, boy! Do you want to work behind a shop-counter? That's all you'll be good for if you don't put your mind to your lessons!"

But admonitions cannot change a romantic into a studious scholar. I simply could not whip up any interest in lessons. Arithmetic seemed something quite beyond my capabilities. Analysis and parsing seemed the dullest thing ever invented. And what did it matter if some plants were dicotyledonous and some monocotyledonous as we were taught in Nature Study? Who wanted to know where Ullswater and Derwentwater were? What did it matter in which year Edward the First began to reign and which year he ceased to reign? History and Geography seemed to have no point whatever. In Dictation I was pretty all right; my spelling was passable. And in Drawing—well, that was just second nature, as I have already mentioned. No one could complain that I was no good at that. On the whole, I simply did not care if I went to school or not. The very word school depressed me.

The one consolation was the heroic fantasy I had woven around my school companions and myself. I looked forward to meeting the members of my "secret society" and giving them instructions for the day's moves, and discussing with them our latest successes in outwitting the enemy gang.

Also, there was stamp-collecting. Going to school gave me the opportunity of exchanging stamps with the other boys. I became friendly with an East Indian girl, Kathleen R—— who was interested in stamp-collecting, too, and we discussed stamps and exchanged one or two specimens. I did not fall for her, though. But I did for her sister—a younger sister called Irene. In fact, so much did Doctor Wang Fu become enamoured of Irene that he named one of his valuable crystals after her!

One day—I was eleven years old—I heard of Buffalo Bill. I had seen boys with periodicals containing stories about this great hero. The covers always carried lurid pictures of a horseman or horsemen being pursued by fierce Red Indians. Those in the know discussed the doings of Buffalo Bill with great enthusiasm, and this aroused my curiosity. So I went into the book department of S.D. & Co. in the Strand and looked around.

I bought a copy of the latest Buffalo Bill story—and my reading career had begun.

It may seem odd that I had never read even a children's book before the age of eleven, but in those days there was no public library in New Amsterdam, and even if there had been children's books would not have been stocked. No Enid Blyton existed then, nor comic strips. Novels were for grown-ups. My mother and aunts had thrived on Mrs. Henry Wood—*East Lynne* was discussed in reverent tones—and Hall Caine and Marie Corelli. This last pair were deemed literary giants; no one had ever written, nor would ever write, such masterpieces as they had turned out. Their works were sighed over and wept over. And, of course, they were not for children!

No one objected to my reading Buffalo Bill. In fact, it seemed a good sign that I had begun to take an interest in literature, even if it was only literature of a blood-and-thunder kind. Though my grandmother offered me the Bible and an old, worn copy of *Pilgrim's Progress*. For her, Bunyan was the only literary genius who had ever lived. I did make an effort to read *Pilgrim's Progress*, but could not get far in it. It bored me. Buffalo Bill was much more exciting. Buffalo Bill was more in the tradition of Doctor Wang Fu and the serials I saw at the cinema. Elmo Lincoln and Eddie Polo were my kind of men.

So impressed was I by the silent film serials and by Buffalo Bill that a strong desire came alive in me to create heroes of my own in tales as exciting as those enacted on the screen and in the pages of the periodical I loved. I bought an exercise book, and began to write a story.

The popular place for a holiday was the Corentyne Coast, but we had never been able to afford such a luxury. I spent all my summer school-holidays at home. The first of these since my reading career had begun—that would be in August, 1921—I spent in writing my long story. I filled my exercise book with pencilled words in a round hand. The story was divided not into chapters but "episodes", and each episode was divided into Part One and Part Two—exactly as it was done in the silent film serials. The setting was not British Guiana but a wild country somewhere in the world; it lacked a name, but possessed ample prairies and dangerous jungles for good galloping adventures featuring horsemen and gangsters and savages with blowpipes and poisoned arrows. Part One ended on a curtain-incident, and each episode (*i.e.* End of Part Two) concluded on a note of harrowing peril. The hero was lying, bound and gagged, beside a box of dynamite towards which a trail of fire was rapidly creeping. Or he had been cornered by the Master Gangster and his henchmen on the edge of a thousand-foot-high cliff. You simply *had* to read on to discover how he got out of his predicament.

This occupation was rather frowned upon by the Authorities. It was not forbidden, but I was told: "It would be much more profitable if you spent your time looking at your lesson-books." It was sound advice, though I did not think so. When school re-opened my interest in lessons had waned even further. I was so backward that Mother, quite anxious now, decided that a private tutor would have to be found for me to give me extra lessons at home in the evenings.

Tutors were not easy to find—at least, not in the middle-class. Up to as late as the nineteen-thirties only the lower classes aspired to be school-teachers. The few in the middle-class who did go in for teaching either kept very exclusive private-schools or aimed for jobs in one of the secondary schools—and these could be counted on the fingers of one hand. In fact, the only ones I knew of were Queen's College and St. Stanislaus' R.C. School, both in Georgetown, and Berbice High School in New Amsterdam. For girls there was Bishop's High School in Georgetown, and in both Georgetown and New Amsterdam the Roman Catholics ran their convent-schools, extremely exclusive institutions controlled and staffed by the nuns.

Eventually a black gentleman called Mr. Griffith was found for me. He came on two evenings every week and sat with me in the dining-room to teach me how to cope with problems in arithmetic, how to compose good sentences, and how to parse and analyse them. There might also have been some geography and history thrown in; my memory fails me. He was a brilliant man, and did his best—but he was always ill at ease in our home, always gushingly affable and fidgety. He made me fidgety, too—and sleepy.

I dawdled along, making no real progress—and I was forbidden to write any stories during the school term. I was even warned that I would not be allowed to read any Buffalo Bills if I continued to show no improvement in my lessons. Nor must I give my attention to my stamp collection except at weekends.

Meanwhile I was still having a lot of fun at school with the black boys. Apart from the Wang Fu operations, I was being rapidly initiated into the intricacies of sex. There was no reserve about my companions, and they not only talked freely about sex but were often distinctly Rabelaisian. They exposed themselves, comparing size and power of virility—sometimes taking measurements with rulers. We cat-called at girls, and made speculations about the beddable qualities of this or that one. We competed with each other in making lewd drawings.

Every noon and every afternoon, at about four, we heard the tinkle of many bicycle bells and the chorus of voices that meant that the boys from the high-school—Berbice High School—about a quarter of a mile farther north along the road, were on their way home. Privileged boys. Boys whose parents could afford to pay the nine dollars per term for their education. Among them was the son of the dentist, John Davis, who had attended Geneva Academy with me. Now and then we met to exchange stamps, but, on the whole, he moved in a sphere unfamiliar to me. He mixed with he-boys who played back-yard cricket and who went exploring in the savannah lands behind the Race Course. They swam in a pond at a place called Cow Dam. Once I had asked my mother if I could go with Johnny and his friends to Cow Dam.

"What! To bathe in that pond! Do you want to get drowned, boy? Oh, no! Nothing of the sort! Don't ever let me hear you say you want to go there!"

All this and more poor Doctor Wang Fu had to swallow!

PLATE 2 A swarthy baby — one year old

PLATE 3 David Leblanc—after a photograph taken in 1901 when he was on a visit to London

PLATE 4 Rebecca Leblanc (née Downer) — with Bible in hand

PLATE 5 My mother when she was 19

PLATE 6 My father — in old age

PLATE 7 My mother — in middle age

PLATE 8 Pastor John Robert Mittelholzer — after a painting (artist unknown) executed in 1870 when he was in a Lutheran seminary in Baltimore, U.S.A.

Chapter Twelve

1922

WE ALL have our Years. Just as nations and the world at large remember certain notable years—1066, 1815, 1914—we must each of us individually see on the private screens of our memories the years that made history for us in particular. 1922 is one of my Years.

It could not have been February when the Authorities announced that I must begin attending Confirmation Classes.

I had known about baptism. More popularly, christenings. But confirmation? The term baffled me. So far, my only contact with any church had been the Lutheran Church where Sunday School was held from half-past two to four. There I had sat with dozens of other children and been talked at into a light doze about the same old Bible stories I had heard from my grandmother. Adam and Eve. Noah and the Flood. The Tower of Babel. Samson. Head lurching, eyes blinking open and relentlessly shutting again, I had listened and dutifully absorbed the philosophy of the Sermon on the Mount. Been hazily impressed by the Miracles and St. Paul and his travels. Had accepted the Crucifixion and the Resurrection because I was told to. And believed everything would be sorted out on Judgment Day—wings and milk and honey for all who read the Bible, loved God, and went to church on Sunday; and for the Others that well-deserved perpetual sizzling in Satan's roomy underground oven.

The word confirmation, however, I was certain, had never been mentioned. In the Lutheran Church, as I later discovered, you were "received", not "confirmed". They had pastors but no bishops. And attending classes in the Anglican Church, I began to learn that "pastor" was a term at which one's nose ought to lift slightly. The really respectable church dignitaries were bishops, priests, deacons, and, indeed, even archdeacons, deans, canons and archbishops! Confirmation was "the laying on of hands". It was a minor miracle performed by a bishop who, having been ordained a bishop by another bishop, had acquired the power to communicate with the Holy Ghost direct Who, in turn, and on request, transmitted that particular divine spark necessary to make one a member of the Church of England. It was something Lutherans, Presbyterians, Wesleyans and Congregationalists went to their graves without having. All because they lacked bishops!

I felt cosy. Now, at last, I was being initiated into something really safe and significant. There was romance in it. And the man who made it seem safe, significant and romantic was the Rector who himself took the classes. The Reverend Mr. Ernest Jones, M.A. (Oxon). An Englishman.

Like my grandmother, he was a man of imagination—and a raconteur. Of medium height, with the suggestion of a stoop, fair, with alert, keen, rather grey than blue eyes, he had a habit of moving his head from side to side in quick comprehensive jerks, as though taking in everything and everyone within range in camera-detailed completeness. And the rimless pince-nez he wore aided, rather than hindered, this process, you felt. Yet there was nothing forbidding about him. On the other hand, he had a smile that instantly disarmed and charmed; there was humour in it, and kindliness, and, often, utter sentimentality. He told everything in a convincing voice, and illustrated it with anecdotes that were interesting if not necessarily very original; in fact, some of them sounded so flat as to make us fidget with discomfort—a discomfort engendered chiefly by the sentimental note in his voice and his sudden blinking stare, and sometimes, too, by the frequent "What! What!" at the end of a sentence, an English upper-class affectation which I had already begun to be familiar with in the speech of the boys of St. Frank's. For my cousin, Victor Jones, had introduced me to the Nelson Lee Library. ("Begad! What a spiffing scheme!" . . . "Just what I thought, dear boy. Perfectly top-hole, what!")

John Davis was a member of this Confirmation Class, and we always sat together. I called for him on my way to the church. We were both very keen. Apart from the personality of the Rector ("call me Rector or Father," he told us from the outset, "not Mr. Jones!"), the doctrines as propounded to us took our fancy. We never wanted to doze, and listened to every word. We discussed it afterwards, and when the Rector asked questions, as he frequently did, we proved to be among his most brilliant pupils.

Classes had not long been in session when the Rector called John and myself and another boy, Harold B——, into the vestry to tell us something. He wanted us to begin training to be altar-servers! Yes, he had chosen us specially because we seemed intelligent boys—and more than that! Here he bent towards us confidentially. "It's not everyone who can be an altar-server. I choose my boys because of their characters!" And, further, he wanted respectable boys. No riff-raff! Even at that age, I could sense the great gush of snobbery pouring from his earnest face. And it affected me. I could feel myself being better than the riff-raff. Here was something to be lived up to! It was not every day one heard this kind of flattery. At home and at school, one was made to feel that one was inadequate, even a little good-for-nothing runt. But here was the Rector singling one out as first-class material, choosing one to be an altar-server! It was a revolution in values. I agreed with solemn enthusiasm to do my best. So did John. So did Harold.

So besides the classes we had to attend, there was the mystery of the vestry. And the vestments. And the Vessels.

This was a chalice and this a paten. Here was a chasuble and here an alb. *This* was worn over the sleeve, and was called a maniple. The left arm, remember! And these stoles were of different colours. Why? Each was for a different season. Like the altar-cloth, did you notice? White for Easter. Purple for Lent and Advent. Green for the Trinity. Red for Saint Days and important Feast Days. I learnt what was a reredos and at what season the paschal-candle was lit. What I would have called a decanter at home I now heard called a flagon. There were two, one for wine and one for water. And this object looked like three bicycle bells in a cluster with handle for holding, but it was one bell—the sacristy-bell.

It was a truly colourful, fascinating world I found myself

being led into, and my head spun with delight. The purple cassock and the lace-frilled surplice I was told I would have to wear did make me recoil somewhat. Memories of the puffy silk bow came growling up. The idea of lace, especially, seemed unbearably effeminate for the tough, wily Doctor Wang Fu. But the other altar-boys wore this get-up. Johnny and Harold were going to wear it, so I probably would be able to get used to it, too.

I did. And on the big day—the 25th of June—I wore my purple cassock and lace surplice, as did Johnny and Harold, and knelt before the bishop for the laying on of hands. For the three of us there was an extra cachet in the occasion. Apart from the fact that we were the only three candidates in sacristan costume, the Bishop actually altered his language for our benefit. Instead of saying "Defend, O Lord, this thy child Edgar," he said: "Defend, O Lord, this thy servant Edgar." It was the first time for me, that the word "servant" had seemed imbued with an aura of distinction. After the service, I felt—just as the Rector said we all would—like an entirely different person. I was now a boy full of grace. I had been washed clean of all sin, and had had my whole being charged with that special pure something that only a bishop could bring down from heaven. Doctor Wang Fu was dead.

On week-days—generally Tuesdays and Thursdays—St. Edgar attended the plain mass at a quarter to eight in order to practise how to serve at the altar. Plain mass was celebrated at the small altar in the Lady Chapel, and while Matins was being said it was the duty of the server to light the candles and take the wine and water flagons to the little table beside the tall side-screen. These simple tasks became surrounded with a pink glow of romance. I would not have shared them with anyone. In fact, for the whole operation I cultivated an obsessive possessiveness. It would have been a disaster if for some reason I had been told that I was not required to serve on any particular morning. Among us servers a fierce competition arose. Whose turn was it this Sunday to be torch-bearers? Whose was it to serve? And whose was it to be right-hand server? There was a hierarchy among us. Eric R—— and Conway who had been servers before the advent of Johnny, Harold and myself, claimed seniority. At sung eucharist, the pukka event of the day, four of us were required—two to carry the candle-standards; the torch-bearers—and two to serve the officiating priest. Torch-bearers were just a cut beneath servers at this big service. And the server at the right-hand side of the altar was the one who had the more important tasks to do, so he was a cut above the server on the left. Therefore every Sunday Eric R——, as the most senior, claimed it as his right to function on the right. It was he, too, who chose whom he wanted to serve with him, so automatically the remaining two had to be torch-bearers.

At evensong there was competition, too. The servers had chairs reserved specially for them in the choir stalls. The chair nearest the priest was the chair of honour, and the senior server occupied this. Just to sit in it alone gave one prestige above his fellow-servers. But there was another honour to be won before the service came to an end. One boy had to go up to the altar, fetch the large silver plate and come down and collect the bags of money from the sidesmen after the offertory, then take it up to the altar to the priest. A lot of genuflecting was involved in this operation, hence a lot of notice from the congregation and a lot of kudos. If there was a procession on a big feast day, more honours were available. Apart from torch-bearers—and on this occasion torch-bearers rose in status—two boys were needed to be cope-bearers. Opinions were divided on the question of kudos. The torch-bearers seemed to attract a lot of attention—and not only from the congregation but from the cluster of sightseers at the various entrances of the church. Yet wasn't it a greater honour to be holding the Rector's cope and walking right beside him?

Inevitably quarrels resulted, and the Rector ruled that everything would have to be arranged in advance. Hence came into being The Rota. This was a list made out by the Rector who decided who was to serve when and where and who to be torch-bearers and cope-bearers. And being a man steeped in snobbery, despite his other sound qualities, he often saw to it that John or myself or Harold got the plums. In fact, he went further than this. At the end of evensong on an Easter Sunday or some other Sunday when the following day was a bank holiday, he would come and whisper to Johnny or myself: "I want you to come with me to Deutichem tomorrow.'' Or it might be Sandvoort. This meant that he was making a trip to one of the small country churches and needed a server. It meant a car journey which alone was worth the whole undertaking—at least, from my point of view.

The following day I would appear at the Rectory, and would be introduced to a lady, a friend of his and his wife's, who had been asked to accompany us on the journey. Invariably he uttered his clucking snob-sounds and added: ''One of my best servers. Comes of one of the oldest families in the colony. What! What!'' And his wife—her name was Maud—would smile widely, pleasantly but noncommittally. He and she were extremely devoted. They went everywhere together. She always accompanied us on these trips.

I don't care two hoots about his little snobbish ways; like every human being, it was inevitable that he would be flawed in some fashion. At core he was good. He was active in the parish, scolded and out-stared those of his flock who came to the Rectory with thin hard-luck tales—but never failed to help them. I know of at least two old servants of ours who used to come and tell us about his good deeds, and of the visits he and his wife paid to the homes of the back-pew members and the interest he took in their affairs—an interest that was not merely perfunctory and dutiful; action always followed his visits. Help was given to those who really deserved it.

There were two trust funds that the Rector of All Saints controlled—the Pattoir Fund and the Douglas Fund. Two rich merchants, earlier in the century, had left their money to be used for the benefit of impoverished church-members. It was in the Rector's discretion to disburse this money as he saw fit.

I was engaged in writing my summer-holiday exercise-book-long story when I began to hear about the Douglas Fund. The Authorities threw out hints of some big plan that was being discussed, and the Rector was mixed up in it. There seemed to be serious doubt as to whether it was the proper thing to accept some offer. And it had to do with me and school. At length, it was considered appropriate to take me into their confidence. I was informed that the Rector had very kindly offered to pay my fees at the high-school out of the Douglas Fund. Did I realise what this meant? . . . ''Your father can't afford to send you to high-school, but the Rector wants you to have a secondary education. He insists that you must be sent to high-school. But it's up to you to work hard and show him that the money is being well spent. Are you going to make an effort to work hard at your lessons?" . . . And so forth . . . Of course, I would work hard, I promised. At high-school! Johnny went to high-school. And all the other boys on their bicycles. Yes, of course, I would work hard . . . "In order to get a good Government job you must hold at least a Junior Cambridge Certificate. It's no use applying to the Government unless you pass that examination. If you don't have that certificate it means you'll have to work behind a shop-counter. Do you realise that? You have to have ambition, boy. I don't know what is to become of you if you don't work harder at your lessons . . ."

Again, it will be noted, from my mother came these admonitions. In fact, I am fairly sure that whatever conferences were held over the project she must have been the one who took the leading part from our home. Even though Dad, at this time, was already a sidesman and church-warden—eventually he became the Rector's Warden—he was so retiring and self-effacing in his general attitude that I am doubtful whether he would have had the courage to discuss such a "delicate" matter as this. And both he and Mother must have considered it extremely delicate. School-fees for a son of theirs to be paid out of a charitable fund! My aunts and grandmother, too, must have had to be consulted. Could Mittelholzer-Leblanc pride withstand such an onslaught? Perhaps what brought matters to a head was the very indifference of my father. I remember quarrels at about this time in the course of which Mother accused him of not caring what happened to me. He had more than once thrown out hints that I should look for work—"get into harness" was his favourite phrase. Lover of words and Latin, spare-time artist, Christmas short-story writer, he of all people, one would have thought, should have been eager to see me advance scholastically. But he shrugged the matter off. And this was not because of the swarthiness of my complexion; he was equally as indifferent about my two younger brothers, both fair-complexioned; he lavished sentimental attentions upon them right into their late teens, much to their embarrassment, but he took no interest whatever in their education.

However, as he himself might have put it if he had been writing this, *jacta alea est*!

Yes, the die had been cast. Next September, when the new school-year began, in this very year, 1922, I would enter the Berbice High School as a new boy.

Chapter Thirteen

HIGH SCHOOL AND NELSON LEE

THE CANADIAN MISSION, evidently under the impression that British Guiana was just another tropical country, a heathen land, like parts of Africa or India where the Natives were in "crying need" of the Gospel of Christ, had in 1915 or 1916, founded "a mission-school" in Berbice for the sons of peasant East Indians, especially the East Indians on the Corentyne Coast—the strip of territory along the north-eastern seaboard between the mouths of the Berbice and Corentyne Rivers. The school-building was used as a church on Sundays. It was situated in a large expanse of land on the extreme northern edge of the town, and within the same grounds stood several other buildings, two of which were used as dormitories for the East Indian boys from the Corentyne; they were the only boarders.

Eventually the Canadian Mission had thrown the school open to all-comers, and when I started out as a pupil in September, 1922, the boys were a mixture of every class, creed and race in the colony. Anglican Chinese, Roman Catholic Portuguese, Hindu-Moslem-into-Christian East Indians, black boys of Wesleyan, Presbyterian, Anglican or Congregationalist origin, and Coloured middle-class boys ditto. The masters had originally been Canadians only, but now there were olive-skinned local-born masters as well as Canadian. On my arrival I found as Headmaster the Reverend Mr. George Rattee (Rats) and a Mr. MacNeil, Canadians, also Mr. Bannister (Banny) and Mr. Parkinson (Parky), olive-skinned locals.

I think that what impressed me most was the fact that here was no chanting, squalling mass of boy-and-girl humanity as at the free school, no murmuring easy-going casualness as at P.A.'s and Mr. Adams's establishments. Here there was silence—and discipline. Everything had a clockwork precision of functioning that appealed to my innate sense of orderliness. I began to realise that where the other schools had failed as an attraction for me was in their lack of organisation; things had been run on too chaotic a basis. In this new school you knew exactly what subject you were going to be taught at exactly what hour, and you knew what master was going to take the class. A bell rang at the end of every period. I could respond to such a system—and I did respond. I began to take an interest in lessons for the first time in my life. Like my altar-serving, lessons began to take on an aura of romance. I wanted to please the masters by doing good work. One got marks in class; there was competition. Therefore I resolved to get as many marks as possible and be among the top three or four boys. Unlike at the other schools, arithmetic was taught simply and in a way that struck straight at the reason; not merely as something that involved a mass of formulae to be memorised parrot-fashion. I began to like arithmetic.

The masters commanded respect in a way that the masters at the other schools had not. P.A. used to walk around with his cane, stern, questing, on the alert for slackness and negligence. Mr. Adams had remained a background figure, charming but indifferent, whiningly querulous when you were taken before him for some misdemeanour. At this school, only the Headmaster used the cane—and only on rare occasions when a boy had been sent to him. Here the masters seemed more interested in imparting knowledge than in being executives or disciplinarians. Moreover, they were individuals. Each was a Character. Mr. Rattee, tall, blue-eyed, with a narrow face and a weak smile, had an acid-drop manner; one instant he was being very soft and sweet, the next he was oozing acidulity in look, smile and voice. Mr. MacNeil, young, shortish, solidly built, looked like a boxer rather than a schoolmaster, and he behaved like one, too; brisk, active, cheerful, controlled in his movements. Mr. Bannister, of medium height and build, had an attractive smile, a quietly confident manner, and a Barbadian accent (a melodious mixture of Surrey, Welsh, Scotch and Irish impossible to imitate). Mr. Parkinson, thin, medium in height, with alert grey-brown eyes that pin-pointed every detail of a scene as they stared through rimless pince-nez, was a vibrant, dynamic sort of man; you could feel his vibrations tingling around you the moment he entered the class-room. His voice was like his manner, crisp, clear, commanding, military. He was always erect, and he was always encouraging us to sit erect. His favourite trick was to approach from behind, clap his hand on the back of your neck and snap: "Sit up, sleepy! Sit up!"

The boys, silent and orderly during class hours, were noisy and rough at recess-time and before the bell rang in the morning and at one o'clock. They ragged me—and "initiated" me; stood in a ring around me and hurled me about as though I were some kind of cloth-ball. Fortunately the era of the Umbrella was over. Mother did not insist on my protecting myself from the weather on the way to school, even though the journey was nearly double that I used to make to any of the other schools. I am sure my life would have been quite impossible if I had been forced to use an umbrella.

Long before the end of term I had lost any strangeness I had felt at first and had made friends with my form-mates. My old sense of inadequacy lessened, but did not vanish, because one or two adverse factors were still in operation. The boys discussed their activities at week-ends, savannah explorations and swims in ponds and canals, but I had to keep silent, because I was not permitted to join them. Also, most of them had bicycles, but I had none; my parents could not afford to give me one. To counter-balance these disadvantages, however, I could hold my own with the best of them in class. I did very well in the terminal examinations. Topped in several subjects, tied in Arithmetic and Geometry—about three of us got 100 per cent—and came second or third in the form as a whole. The Authorities, for the first time, were able to pay me a few compliments on my performance.

I won new liberties in respect to reading and writing. No one tried to forbid me from settling down with a Nelson Lee, or warned me to pay more attention to my lessons than I gave to writing silly stories.

Nelson Lees had become far more important to me now than Buffalo Bills. In fact, I had outgrown Buffalo Bill. Nowadays I preferred to read of the adventures of the boys of St.

Frank's College. This exclusive school "for the sons of gentlemen" assumed a solid realness not only for me but also for my good chum Johnny, and later for several of the other boys to whom I introduced the periodical. Published weekly by the Amalgamated Press, these stories were written by someone who was nameless at first. But they became so popular, evidently in England and in other countries of the British Empire as well as in New Amsterdam, that the publishers decided to reveal their authorship. Thus we Nelson Lee fans suddenly discovered that we had to thank a chap called Edwy Searle Brooks for the school and its familiar personalities—Nelson Lee, detective turned house-master but still as astute as when he practised in London, outwitting the best criminal brains, remained perpetually in the background, only now and then having a word or two with Nipper, his assistant, now one of the boys of the Remove. Then there were Handforth and his two study-mates, Church and MacClure, and Sir Monty and Watson, and Archie Glenthorne who stuttered and exclaimed: "Gadzooks!" and wore a monocle. And the cads, Fullwood and Co., who broke bounds to go off to Bannington to smoke and gamble. The nearby village was called Belton, and there was a wood where sometimes strange and sinister events occurred. Master-criminals out for Nelson Lee's blood were apt to lie in ambush in it.

So real and exciting was this world that Johnny and I spoke of it as though it was a place we one day hoped to visit. We imitated the speech of the boys of St. Frank's, and soon had a lingo of our own in which such words as "spiffing", "top-hole", "beastly", "frightful", "sneak", "bunk!" (for "Run off! Get out!") became part of our casual, everyday vocabulary. No wonder that when I depicted two middle-class youths in my novel, *Corentyne Thunder*, who spoke like this, the publishers, in accepting it, had to remark in their list of "minor flaws": "Pages 90 and 103. The very unreal conversation between Geoffrey and Stymphy . . . Half-caste youths don't speak like old Uppinghamians."

Chapter Fourteen

MYTH AFTER MYTH

AS WE GROW up we progress from myth to myth, and each myth has its sustaining value. In quick retrospect I can sense the fascination of the stereoscope and its collection of pictures at "Rosedale", the carriage trip to Cumberland, Uncle Bishop and his bees and bush-relics and lore of wild living, the evening visits of the Fraser children and of Ivy and Maud C——, the saw-mill and the music of the Olympic cinema, Gwen and *Daisy*, *Daisy*, the Luckhoos and the Corentyne Coast, Buffalo Bill, and then the Church and altar-serving, Nelson Lee and the boys of St. Frank's. I am almost forgetting to include Doctor Wang Fu and the wind-humming noons at P.A.'s school. The older I grew the greater the hold of the myth on me.

The Church had a long run, and so had Nelson Lees, which were soon joined by Sexton Blakes. The adventures of Sexton Blake and Tinker were featured both in the Sexton Blake Library and in a periodical called *Union Jack*. Johnny and I clubbed funds and subscribed to both. We got them at first through the book-department of S.D. & Co. Later we subscribed direct from the Amalgamated Press.

High-school was, in its way, another myth—and yet another came to enmesh me. A new Scout troop was formed under the Scoutmastership of a very popular man of the middle-class, a Mr. Muss. In accordance with the regulations, every Scout troop had to have a number, and this troop was Number Forty-nine. But it was no common or garden troop. It was an élite troop for the sons of gentlemen, therefore Mr. Muss decided that it must have a name as well as a number. Lady Davson, wife of Sir Edward Davson, Bart., was asked to be the Patroness. She agreed, so the troop was named Lady Davson's

Own. A temporary club-room was established in a cottage in Queenstown, not very far from where my Aunt Elfreda and her family lived—Queenstown is a purely residential section of the town, north of the Promenade Garden, and features many bungalows and two-storied dwellings in spacious gardens, and many mosquitoes and sand-flies, for it is very bushy. News of the manly, Scout-like things that went on in this club-room began to reach me at school through Johnny, who had already joined up, and other boys in my own Form One. I was always being shown lengths of cord and witnessing the tying of a variety of knots. I heard about Kim's Game—a sort of observation test—and about fire-lighting, and even camping. I threw out powerful hints at home that I should like to join, knowing, however, what the reaction would be in advance. "You're not accustomed to camping out in the open. And these boys, I hear, go swimming in canals and ponds. And, in any case, you'll have to have a uniform. I can't afford that."

But I continued to hint. And then Mr. Muss, man of charm, spoke to my mother when he met her on some social occasion, and his charm seemed to work, for I detected a weakening in her attitude.

The subject was discussed by the Female General Staff. My grandmother was in favour—which did not surprise me, for she herself had never tried to mollycoddle me. In fact, every now and then, in a subtle effort to counteract my mother's soft-egg policy towards me, Grandma would recount her own girlhood escapades—tomboy activities in the open air: climbing trees and swims in punt-canals. Because of her incapacity through the loss of her leg, she had to be careful nowadays what she said; inactive in body, with a highly active mind and spirit, she found life irksome and frustrating: indeed, she suffered tortures during those latter years. She had to employ a tinsel-delicate ingenuity in her efforts to sustain an atmosphere of harmony between herself and her daughters. On several occasions she would have liked to support one of my causes, but had she done this too strongly it would have been interpreted as "interference" by my mother and resulted in a bitter, petty squall of words, with my aunts gustily joining in. In order barely to exist at all she had to possess the diplomatic tact of a skilled Foreign Office official.

I can't remember exactly how my aunts responded, but eventually the reluctant decision was made that I could join. "But bear in mind that I'm making no promise about your uniform! You can attend the meetings, but you'll have to wait until I can afford to give you a uniform."

So the new myth came alive and spread new colours through my imagination. I attended the club-meetings in Queenstown and learnt to tie knots like the other boys—reef, bowline, sheep-shank—and discovered the uses of a stave, was taught how to signal with my arms and how to tap out the Morse Code, how to do the Scout Pace—walk twenty, run twenty. I took my Tenderfoot Test and passed.

After much plotting, pleading, postponement and harrowing suspense, my uniform became, at last, an actuality. And my knife, whistle, lanyard.

And one shining day we gathered at Davson House to receive our Tenderfoot Badges from Lady Davson who happened to be on one of her periodical visits to the colony. We had rehearsed for this ceremony for weeks, and were all keyed up and tense.

Davson House stood in spacious grounds, well kept to the last blade of grass on its immaculate lawns. It had a bottom-house like any other house, but it was a *paved* bottom-house. We formed up on this paved bottom-house, and Mr. Muss ran us through one grand final rehearsal. We had to pretend that he was Lady Davson and walk up to him one by one and salute smartly. Then he pretended to pin on the badge, and another smart salute, about turn, march back to the line . . . "Don't sway your shoulders, Mittelholzer! You're not in the Navy. You're not a sailor on leave. Back into line and do it again!" A sniggering in the ranks. Mittelholzer returns into line and tries again . . . "Much better! Much better!"

Our troop came first in a competition among all the troops in the colony. In a parade we stood out, for our uniform was distinctive. Other troops, without exception, wore navy-blue shorts and khaki shirts. Our uniform was khaki throughout. Other troops had scarves of two colours—blue and green, or blue and red, or black and yellow. Our scarves were of one colour—lemon yellow. Other troops, without exception, were composed of boys of chocolate-brown complexions, spotted here and there with a light-brown or olive. Our troop was olive, with many touches of pink.

Came the day when there was heard a great wailing and a miserable gnashing of teeth on the part of one member of Lady Davson's Own. It was the time when the first big camp was arranged. This member was informed by his mother that he definitely could not go. "What! On the Corentyne Coast to sleep in the open air!"

"In tents, Mother."

"I don't care. You're not accustomed to such a thing. Do you want to contract tuberculosis?"

Mr. Muss intervened, oozing charm and reassurance. There was a wavering, a dithering, within the fortress. Loyalties divided sharply on the issue. Ominous silences and rumbling quarrels moved like thunder-clouds in the rafters. Up to the very last hour it was in doubt whether I would go or not.

I did not. I sat under the mango tree on the western side of the house and watched the lorry-load of boys go past in the Strand, vanishing and appearing between the trees in the Luckhoos' yard until it got to the saw-mill when it vanished for good. The troop was on its way to the perils of the Corentyne Coast, leaving one member of the Rattlesnake Patrol behind, safe in his dark-raftered Coburg Street home that faced the police-station *and* the fire-station!

Not even a Nelson Lee or a Sexton Blake could counter the bitterness of that disappointment. It left a deep stain on my memory—but, as always, a neutral one. No moment of disappointment has ever left a positive mark on my character. My resilience—the resilience with which I was born—unfailingly absorbed the colour of these adverse moments. I can look back on them without rancour—with smiling detachment. They are like interesting shadows lying across the trail of events that go to make up my past: shadows painted by a Courbet rather than a Seurat or Camille Pissarro.

Chapter Fifteen

MYTH AND ANTI-MYTH

CHRISTMAS was another myth that continued to provide a lot of sustenance. Father Christmas—we seldom called him Santa Claus—had faded from the picture since I was about nine or ten. The Luckhoo boys and I had discovered the hoax. But though we missed hanging up our stockings on Christmas Eve, there were still the Masqueraders to look forward to throughout the whole season. Small groups of men and women, of the proletariat only, wore masks and went about the town with flutes and drums accompanied often by a Mother Sally figure who provided most of the fun whirling and jigging. In passing, they would pause to send a representative into the gateway, and it was the customary thing to throw a coin down to him, or, at least, let the servant take down some ginger-beer for the group. It was always exciting for us children to listen for the drums approaching and to speculate whether the masqueraders would turn down our street or simply pass on along Main Street or the Strand. Occasionally members of the middle-class condescended to masquerade, but this was done in the evening when it was dark, and it consisted only of wearing a costume and mask and going about and calling on one's friends. Quite unlike the vulgar Trinidadians who "play masque" in the streets all day at Carnival time! It was not until I was in my mid-twenties that I even understood what Carnival was. All that happened in Guiana on Shrove Tuesday was that we ate pancakes.

Writing, of course, turned out to be the Myth That Never Died. Faithfully every summer holiday—though we called it August holiday; in Guiana summer lasts all the year round—I sat down to write my exercise-book-ful of exciting story. It was probably in 1923 that I did *The Trail of the Coloured*

Flints which featured, I recall, a character referred to as Lal Sonfra's Missionary, a mysterious masked horseman who came to the rescue of the hero and his party whenever they were in any strikingly perilous situation—and such a situation unfailingly occurred at the end of each episode. It was in an exercise book with a shiny red cover that the small, neat words in lead pencil were written, and for at least two years afterwards I was still passing it round among my school-fellows. There is a diary entry to this effect. *SUNDAY*, *1st February*, 1925: "Went to Mass 8 a.m. and 11 a.m. Went for a stroll with John in night. Lent Eric Rich. 'Trail of Col. Flints'."

It was late in 1922 or early in 1923 that I began keeping a diary. The first two consisted of small yellow-covered notebooks. Then in 1924, at a church bazaar in the Town Hall—always held on the first Monday in December—I won, as a prize for fishing up a celluloid duck from a miniature pond, a real diary. It had spaces, each about three inches by an inch, allotted for all the days of the year, and was contained within a cover that was really a wallet of imitation Morocco leather. Stamped in gold letters on this cover were the two words WHITE HORSE, though an attempt had been made to paint them out—in gold paint—but without much success. One must assume that whisky advertisements and church bazaars had been looked upon by the lady who had arranged the duck-pond as a rather improper association of ideas.

Every day, without fail, throughout 1925, I wrote briefly about what I had done or experienced, and this habit continued, without my missing a single day, until the fourteenth of May, 1936, when a Certain Event caused me to resolve never to keep a diary again—a resolve I kept until the first of March, 1948.

I still have these diaries, all except the first yellow-covered ones which, somehow, must have slipped away with the moths or the dustman.

Another event that also entered the category of Myth was the coming to New Amsterdam of the Militia Band. It was a magic occasion, and being right opposite to the police-station, I was able to savour the full magic. I was able to stare across at the barracks and watch the bandsmen moving about and talking, and hear them sounding out their instruments. Then at a quarter to five in the afternoon, in their immaculate uniforms, they went marching off west along the street, bound for the bandstand on the Esplanade,[1] just across the road bordering the Promenade Garden. Crowds of nurses and children gathered there, with long lines of cars along the road, for it was only about twice a year that the band visited the town. It was a gesture of condescension from the superior Georgetown, the ten-foot-below-sea-level garden-city where everything was vaster and more up-to-date than in "Berbicetown". In the evenings, the crowds were bigger, and the lines of cars longer, and it was in the evenings that we boys had a really exciting time. We did not go to listen to the music, but to play "catcher"—an impromptu game that took the form of dodging about among the crowds and trying to locate each other at agreed upon intervals. I am certain we must have been a thorough nuisance to the genuine music-lovers.

In contrast to these Magic Moments there was the haunting grim Anti-Myth of the Calomel Capsule.

My sister and I suffered years of mental torture from this pharmaceutical spectre. It threw its shadow on every holiday-period. The longer the holiday the darker the threat of the spectre's shadow. Our mother believed firmly in her fallacies. Nothing could shake her faith. The human system, she was convinced, needed a clean-out at regular intervals, and this clean-out had to be a thorough one. Only calomel could do a thorough job. So whenever holidays began my sister and I steeled ourselves against the announcement that we knew had to come, early or late.

"Edgar! Lucille! Capsules to-night!"

Nestling neatly amidst cotton-wool in a white pill-box were the two torpedo-shaped capsules. They looked like objects more suitable for insertion into some electric fuse than for gulping down into a human stomach. Invariably it stuck at the back of the throat, even when chased with water. Then when it did slip down you could feel it slowly, grittily, ticklingly, travelling every nauseous millimetre of the way stomachwards. You sat, tense, with narrowed eyes and tightly clasped hands, waiting for it to lose itself deep inside you, fighting off the quaking efforts of your stomach to reject it, because

[1] *See* Appendix 4.

you knew that if you brought it up, the whole ordeal would have to be re-enacted twenty-four hours hence. Sometimes, in spite of one's earnest and determined strivings, it did come up. But assuming that you won the encounter and it stayed down, you lay cautiously in bed, still tense but vaguely triumphant; it was no use feeling that you were out of the woods, because you knew that on the following morning another phase of the ordeal awaited you. A large dose of castor oil. Or a nasty half-cup of epsom salts. For calomel had to be "washed out" of the system; a strong purgative was essential on the morning after. So at seven or eight, or earlier, you were awakened, and sitting up in bed, your stomach still very uneasy after a night of calomel activity, you had to reach out and take the castor oil or salts proffered and face yet another duel with your shuddering stomach.

With all this behind you, you would have thought that the reward of a few tasty food-offerings was well deserved. No such luck! You were cautioned: "Now, remember! No sweets or anything with acid for at least three days, or you'll be salivated!" Which meant that all fruit was taboo, for Mother was not the person to take chances. No matter how sweet a fruit, it might just *possibly* contain a slight percentage of acid, so keep away from it. The same applied to manufactured sweets. Furthermore, it would be *fatal* to take a chill when calomel was in your system, so you had to remain indoors for at least two days, no matter how fine the weather. Your pores were open when you took calomel, and a mere *gust* of wind might give you a chill.

As young children, we were made to wear flannel vests. Flannel vests in a climate with the thermometer every day of the year in the eighties. In our teens we were considered old enough, therefore robust enough, to withstand the rigours of the equatorial cold in flannelette.

Each of us has his own conception of freedom. For us in those days, to be free was to be flannel-less and unhaunted by the fear of the Calomel Capsule!

Chapter Sixteen

OUT OF THE MIRE

WHETHER THE Authorities liked it or not, I was gradually crawling out of the mollycoddling mire. My mother and aunts must have realised deep in their repressed beings that I would never conform to their outlook on life. My sister preferred peace at any price, but not so I. The Warrior-tiger kept snapping and snarling, determined not to be smothered.

On the School Front I had won a victory that helped to bolster up my position very considerably. At my first prize-giving I got four prizes—one for topping Form One, one for English, one for Latin and French in the Junior School, and the Principal's Prize, for getting the highest average in marks for the whole school during the preceding year. No longer could I be justifiably scolded for not paying attention to my lessons. I was still cautioned—even scolded—but the sting had gone out of it.

I went to the barber's to have my hair trimmed. Formerly the barber had come to the house, and I had had to sit in a chair in the gallery while he performed. Not that I had minded his visits, because he was a rather pleasant and entertaining man, and he sometimes gave me stamps. Once he asked me to do a drawing for him, and promised me stamps *and* payment. It was a great secret, however. I was to tell no one, nor show anyone the drawing. At that time I was quite ignorant of the aberrations of sex, and it was only afterwards—years afterwards—that I was able to make any sense of his request. The picture he wanted me to draw for him was to be of two men crouching on hands and knees on the floor, and sitting on a raised chair nearby, a full-breasted woman must be shown with her feet resting imperiously on the backs of the men. "They must look subservient, you see." With a furtive glance towards the sitting-room, lest anyone were lurking there who might overhear him; he spoke in a hushed voice, his eyes glittering in an eager way that puzzled me. "You do that for me and I'll give you whatever stamps you want—and two dollars."

I told him I wouldn't take any money—somehow, it seemed improper to take money for a simple drawing—but I would like to have the stamps. I did the drawing, following his instructions and juxtaposing the figures exactly as I had been told to do. He dropped in, as arranged, a week later, and went into ecstasies when he saw the picture . . . "Yes, yes! Just right. Oh, look at that!" He clasped his hands together, sighing, wagging his head, squirming in his effeminate way, completely satisfied.

However, I preferred going to one of the barbers who had shops in various parts of the town. It seemed more manly, and one met interesting characters while one waited. The chatter, too, was worth-while listening to.

I climbed trees. Formerly this had been forbidden . . . "Do you want to fall down and break your neck?" . . . A long pole with a metal hook at the thinner end was used for reaching up into the guava and star-apple trees for picking the ripe fruit. But nowadays I spurned this and climbed into the upper branches myself to get at the fruit. Sometimes I invited Johnny and other chaps at school to come in the afternoon to climb with me. The Authorities uttered disapproving rumbles but took no positive action.

I exposed my body, risking tuberculosis or pneumonia. This happened, however, without the knowledge of anyone at home. When I was at the Scout club-room—a new club-room on the savannah land not far from the Race Course—we would sometimes have to practise tent-building. To do this we had to cut down trees, and as this meant hard work we took off our shirts and sweated away at our tasks. And not only this, but I also discarded my shoes and socks and waded knee-deep across a trench of muddy water to help the other chaps drag some tree-trunks over to the patch of land where our club-room stood. In doing this I was not only risking T.B. and pneumonia but a severe cold in my legs which could result in filaria or elephantiasis. What a sense of daring and freedom I had that day!

At Whitsuntide, 1925, our troop went on another camp, and on this occasion I was allowed to go. For the first time, I was away from home and at the mercy of weather, wild animals and weedy canals. The camp was at a place called Belladrum on the West Coast, Berbice, meaning the flat area of coastland between the mouth of the Berbice River and the mouth of the Abary Creek. Muddy, squelchy terrain—and May is a rainy month. There were lots of canals to get drowned in, but I did not hesitate to take my first plunge with the other boys. They ducked me—an "initiation"—and I emerged spluttering wildly and lunging instinctively for the bank, but having survived this shock, I remained in the water and splashed around and tried to join in the horse-play. Because of the rainy weather and the low, flat terrain, we could not sleep in tents but had to use a school-room. Half the night we spent jabbering at each other and throwing boots, belts and other articles of wear across the dark expanses that separated one patrol from another. On the Bank Holiday Monday we played a cricket match against a village team, but rain kept interrupting play and the match had to be abandoned.

The next great adventure came in October of the same year when once again the Authorities gave their sanction to a perilous hike to a village called Sandvoort on the bank of the Canje Creek. Once again it was in a school-room that we had to sleep, and the following day we crossed the black water of the Creek by boat, and then trudged the three miles back to town along the narrow, red roads—red because they were made up from clay baked red and hard and crushed flat by traffic.

Slowly out of the mire.

In November, the year of adventure was crowned by a trip to Georgetown. Our troop had been invited to take part in a colony-wide competition among Scout troops. I had to do a lot of lobbying and cadging to persuade the Authorities (*a*) that I would survive the pitfalls of city life and (*b*) that the money could be found to finance the project. My diary records: "Got 5/- etc. towards G'town & 2/- more in night." That was on the 2nd of the month. On the 6th I mentioned that I "borrowed blanket & rope from A. Lou. . . . Trying to get *pack* for G'town." Eventually I did go, and survived everything—camp-fires, parades, observation tests, athletics, a tour over a Canadian passenger ship that was in port—I was taken by my cousin Frank, a Customs officer—route marches and tram-car journeys, the firing of the eight o'clock cannon at the old Dutch fort, a custom dating from the days of Slavery—the man who had to do this job allowed us to accompany him; we were temporarily deafened by the sudden roar—visits to my uncle and cousins, shopping in the bustle of Camp Street, a busy commercial street, and walks on the Sea Wall promenade and on the beach beyond it. But on the second night I had to remain within call of the phone. My Aunt Maud, who worked at the Telephone Exchange in New Amsterdam, put through a call to check up. I had to tell her about my adventures, and assure her that my health was still holding out against pneumonia, T.B., filaria and so forth. I had not yet drowned in the Demerara River or in the sea off the Sea Wall.

We slept in hammocks slung up between the walls of an old barrack building at Eve Leary, which is the section of Georgetown noted for military activities. There is a parade ground there, and several barrack-buildings for troops and other military installations. Our old building was near the spot where, in the eighteenth century, the Dutch had built their Fort Willem Frederik, and as I lay in my hammock at five in the morning, I could hear the Reveille coming on the breeze from about half a mile away where the modern buildings stood. An entrancing sound. It was the first time I had heard it *at a distance*. With it was mingled the rhythmical roar of the waves beyond the Sea Wall.

Chapter Seventeen

AN ANNOYING CLOWN

I HAVE NOTHING but sympathy for the masters who had to cope with me at school. I was an annoying schoolboy, perpetually showing off. I had a mania for clowning and indulging in rags. Had anyone tried to predict a career for me he could well have been excused for pronouncing that I would go on the music-hall stage as a comedian. Nothing delighted me more than to say or do something that set the whole form cackling. I drew caricatures of the masters on the blackboard or on slips of paper which I left lying prominently around. I pinned or gummed squares of paper to the backs of the other boys—or to the pigtails of the girls who sometimes came over to join a class from the Girls' School not far away: squares of paper that bore such instructions as KICK ME HARD or CLOUT ME. Sometimes I did happen to perpetrate something with a touch of originality, but, little idiot that I was, instead of resting gracefully on my laurels until the next moment of inspiration, I would immediately try to exploit the situation with a series of quick-fire follow-ups, so that the master, instead of smiling or chuckling as he had done before, told me to write a hundred lines. Mr. Wong, our new Maths master, a Chinese, a man with a sense of humour and a very great deal of patience, once silenced me effectively for a whole afternoon, and he did it quite simply. He had chuckled —while the form cackled—at a quip of mine, but after my second or third attempt to win more laughs, he tilted his head, sighed and said quietly, "Mittelholzer, the point of that joke has now deteriorated. Please shut up."

I caused trouble with crossword puzzles. Over the weekend I would compose a crossword puzzle. I brought it on Monday morning and gave it to the boys to solve. I was not content to supply one copy; I made five or six, so that five or six boys could get busy simultaneously. Lessons were neglected. The masters began to investigate. Miscreants who were caught got lines; persistent offenders were caned.

I invented War Games. We had a sort of a library at our Scout club-room. Among the books there was a set, published, if I remember rightly, by *The Times*: about twelve volumes that gave detailed accounts of the battles of the First World War, together with numerous illustrations. I devoured volume after volume, and my imagination took fire. I could talk about nothing else at school. I recounted some of the stories I had read, and names like Mons and Ypres and Somme and Marne, von Kluck and von Moltke, Foch and Verdun, Joffre and Hill 60 began to be thrown around with casual familiarity. And then I started making paper-pellets of various sizes and bombarding certain "positions". Pellets of a certain size I dubbed Howitzers. Larger ones were Soixante-quinze (i.e. 75 millimetre). Very large ones Big Berthas. Four of us became allies and selected various boys who seemed suitable targets. We gave each a name, Verdun in one case, Hill 60 in another, Huluch-le-Hurlus and so on, and then proceeded to shell these Positions, doing so surreptitiously, however, when the enemy was not expecting an attack. Retaliations followed, and soon a full-scale war was on. Even lines and canings failed to curb the fury of hostilities . . . "Mittelholzer, I saw you pelt that piece of paper!" . . . "I was merely retaliating, sir!" . . . "Very well. Write me a hundred times: 'Vengeance is mine, saith the Lord'."

I sometimes led mango raids. The Presbyterian Manse stood in very spacious grounds, and we had to pass it every day to and from school. All sorts of fruit trees grew in the grounds of the manse, including mangoes of various varieties. Many of these trees were temptingly near the fence. In fact, the branches of one or two actually overhung the ditch that separated fence from grass verge. It was common practice for us to hop across the ditch and help ourselves to any fruit that happened to be within reach. But the best fruit was well inside enemy territory. From the road we could see them, pink and green, in clumps, delicately glimmering in the sunshine. Often I got a tow home on the cross-bar of somebody's bicycle; it might be Johnny or it might be Eric Cossou, the boy who lived next-door in the house that the Eggs once occupied. Three or four bicycles might be moving along abreast, each bearing two. As we neared the Presbyterian Manse the mangoes would come into view, and one of us might suddenly decide that action must be taken. A raid! There was a gap in the fence at one point, a spot where you could duck under the lowest strand of barbed wire. It was here that we broke through the enemy lines and set out on our raid. The minister (at this time a Scotsman, very Scotch, called Mr. Nichols) got in a terrible rage when he happened to see us from his study window, and shouted at us, and we made a scampering, disorderly retreat back to the gap in the hedge. Sometimes he would come down and chase boys, his face as red as his hair. Inevitably he complained to the Principal, and warnings would be issued at morning prayers. But the raids continued—and sometimes the participants were recognised, reported and caned.

I decided one day on a plan which I considered above board. Ironically, however, I caught it literally in the neck. Eric, Cyril Chu, a Chinese boy—both form-mates—and I were on our way home one afternoon when I mooted a mango raid of a somewhat different kind. I suggested our going up to the house and asking the Nicholses for permission to pick some; they would either tell us we could not or point out the worst tree and probably watch us take two or three half-ripe specimens and then order us off. He and his wife were extremely mean with their mangoes. However, I had other ideas in mind; the point was to get permission to pick the fruit; once they gave us permission, off we would dart and make our own selection from the trees we chose. Eric and Cyril hesitated. Who was going to go and ask? I would, I said, and looking virtuous and respectable, the three of us walked along the driveway to the house. I went up the long stairway and knocked on the door. Mrs. Nichols herself appeared. "Can I have some mangoes, please?" I asked. She seemed very surprised, hesitated, then said: "Very well, I'll let you have some." She turned off at once to go inside, and I dashed down to the others and said: "She said yes." Off we streaked to the best trees—the trees that bore the pinkest and most tempting fruit. Swiftly we got to work, and were engrossed in the operation when Cyril suddenly hissed: "Nichols coming! Look!" and dashed off towards the gap in the fence, followed by Eric. I heard a sound like hoof-beats in a cowboy film, turned and saw the Reverend Mr. Nichols galloping towards me, instinctively made to dash off, then stopped. Why should I run? I had asked permission. "I've caught you, you little thief!" panted Mr. Nichols, and grabbed me by the back of my neck. I jerked myself free and said haughtily: "I asked permission. I asked Mrs. Nichols. We weren't stealing them." He barked: "You're a liar! You never asked." This got me angry, and I flung the mangoes I had picked down on to the grass and told him he could keep them. "I did ask. You can go and find out from her if you don't believe me." He recoiled, looking uncertain, then we heard Mrs. Nichols' voice. We went towards the house and she verified that I had asked her for some mangoes. "But I went inside to get them for you." She was holding in her hands two or three ugly-looking green-skinned fruit. "These are what I was bringing to the door to give you, but you'd gone." I told her no thanks, and began to move off. I left them looking a little shame-faced and flustered, and rejoined the other boys on the road. The operation was not an entire failure, because Eric and Cyril had managed to carry off one or two pink-skinned mangoes despite their hasty retreat.

During the Rattee régime canings were frequent. A master would report one of us for an offence, and Old Rats would appear at recess, or perhaps while the lesson was in progress, and in his slithery, whining voice, utter the usual ill-omened intimation: "I'll see you after school!" Actually, he did not use a cane. He had a thin, long leather which he kept in a cupboard in the Senior Room. All appointments were kept in the Senior Room. They were brief and painful, but I think I preferred them to the form of punishment invented by Mr. Wong.

"Mittelholzer! Get on the bench!"

It was not so bad when one had company. But to stand alone on a bench and be stared at by the whole form seemed to me peculiarly humiliating.

On Thursday afternoons we had to attend wood-work class. I was as hopeless as a handyman as I was at cricket and soccer, and found this class a great bore. I merely made a pretence at working. I would spend weeks on planing a few pieces of board, for most of the afternoon would be frittered away in cross-talk with the other chaps, and in various kinds of horse-play. A handful of shavings stuffed down somebody's back unexpectedly was all in the day's casual fun. Missiles, big and small, were perpetually whizzing past our heads. Old Rats himself took these classes, but he was always posted at one end of the long work-room. In shirt-sleeves, he would generally be too busy with the one or two geniuses, sand-papering and glueing bits of wood and turning out cutlery-boxes, breadboards and stools that looked as though they had been produced in a factory—far too busy to notice that a saw-dust bomb had just landed on my shoulder and that I was preparing to hurl one back at the aggressor, or that the sharp clacking report two benches away had resulted from the violent collision between a swiftly sliding hammer and a more swiftly whizzing set-square.

Nature Study classes were often supplemented by practical stints in the open air. A section of the grounds had been apportioned to the Lower School, and we were supposed to keep, two each, a plot of ground in good agricultural order. If we did not actually reach the stage of planting something that grew, the plot must look as though it had been well ploughed, well matured and watered. This was the minimum if disgrace was to be avoided. Eric Cossou and I shared one plot, but half the term passed and it still looked as though it were part of the wilderness of weeds from which it had been won. It had been ploughed by a plough-man at the beginning of term, but Eric and I had spent most of our Nature Study period in observing the effect of pebbles and lumps of earth on the necks and behinds of other boys in the vicinity and in other equally entertaining pursuits. The weeds had, in the meantime, been swift to take advantage of the situation. About two or three weeks before terminal examinations, Banny, who took us in Nature Study, made a swooping inspection of plots, and when he reached ours he exploded . . . "Mittelholzer! Cossou! Do you see the state of this plot! Is this all you've been doing to it for the term?"

"Sir, we've been doing our best with it . . ."

"The weeds grow so fast, sir . . ."

"Very well. If by the time I set the Nature Study papers I find that this plot isn't in a better condition, you'll lose fifty per cent of your marks, just to start with!"

During the next two or three Nature Study periods—and even during lunch-hour and recess—frantic activity. Mittelholzer and Cossou to and fro, from compost heap to plot, with barrow after barrow of manure!

Chapter Eighteen

BARNO

SCHOOL-LIFE for me, in the mid-twenties, was liberally laced with stamp-collecting and Nelson Lees and Sexton Blakes. I mention the latter once again, because my obsession with these periodicals increased instead of diminished. I even indoctrinated at least one grown-up. Eric Cossou had an invalid great-aunt who was permanently bedridden, and he happened to let her read one or two of the Nelson Lees I had lent him. She became a fan, and at regular intervals Eric handed me a few shillings, saying: "This is Aunty's sub. for the N.L.'s." And off would go the postal order to the Amalgamated Press! Readers were requested to write to Edwy Searle Brooks—and I certainly was not going to be left out. I started a brisk correspondence with the poor hard-worked man. He replied not only through the column in the periodical but sometimes personally through the post. Every number received was faithfully recorded in my diary . . . "N.L. No. 518 came . . . Received N.L. No. 522 . . ." On the 25th of June, 1925, I "did not go to morning school. Mouldy day." But to compensate: "N.L. No. 523 came. Wrote letter to Mr. E. S. Brooks. Did not post it. Read N.L." In fact, this was a very bookish day, for in the next line I record: "Also read S.B. Borrowed book from Library (Manco, The Peruvian Chief)."

A very close second for the monotony of its recurrence is "E. & M." These were the initials of a well-known firm of stamp dealers in South Hackney. Messrs. Errington and Martin. Hardly a week went by without my noting that I had received approval sheets from E. & M. or that I had sold some stamps from E. & M.'s sheets to Johnny or Eric or some other boy at school, or that I had posted off a money-order to E. & M. It was through stamp-collecting that I got the nickname that stuck to me, among my very close friends, right up to the present. In *Pearson's Weekly* there used to appear every week, throughout a period of more than two years, a tiny two-line advertisement in the classified section. As far as my memory can be trusted, it ran like this: "*Neurope*—Send 1½d. stamp for 20 Neurope—G. H. Barnet, Lymington, Somerset." I was not particularly interested in European stamps—especially new European ones. British and French colonials were my favourites. But haunted by this advertisement every week—and tempted by the absurd amount asked for—I decided to send three halfpence in stamps and ask for the twenty Neurope. I also showed the advertisement to the boys at school. Several of them took the address eagerly, and at least four of them immediately sent off their three halfpence in stamps. In those days it took about six weeks to get a letter to England and receive a reply, for everything went by sea. Six weeks went by, seven, eight, two months, three months, four months—but none of us heard from G. H. Barnet. It soon became a joke, and I was the one chipped, because it was I who had shown around the advertisement. In revenge they began to call me Barnet. Eventually it was contracted to Barno, and has remained Barno until now.

My interest in Scouting and the Church had by no means waned, however. I went regularly to the club-room to take part in the activities of the troop, sat my Second Class test and passed it, but knew that the possibility of ever becoming a First Class Scout was extremely poor. You had to swim fifty yards in the course of your First Class test, and I could not swim five yards, nor could I foresee any opportunity of learning in the near future. There were no swimming-pools in New Amsterdam, and the river was no good for any kind of bathing. The water was a dirty, muddy amber, and the banks consisted of flat, treacherous stretches of soft, oozy mud infested by crabs. Anyone trying to get into the water *via* the bank of the river would be waist-deep in the mud before he had proceeded ten yards, and with large and small crabs nibbling affectionately, or maliciously, at his ribs. In the meantime I interested myself in signalling, cooking over an open fire lit with not more than two matches and built up entirely of leaves and twigs, tent-building, painting pictures for the club-room and insignias for the flags of the patrol-leaders—an owl for the Owls, a dove for the Doves, a rattlesnake for the Rattlesnakes, my own patrol. And there were the library and, sometimes, church-parades. While the other members of the troop were taking their seats in the pews, Barno and Fisky (as I used to call Johnny at this time; it was an abbreviated corruption of his middle name, Pietzcker) went into the vestry and changed into their purple cassocks and white lace surplices—and then up to the altar with the Rector and the torch-bearers as the hymn for the Introit was being sung. Both of us had now risen in the hierarchy of sacristans. At sung Eucharist we invariably served. Our torch-bearing days were behind us. We used to take particular pleasure in baiting and ousting a short, effeminate chap called Conway. He was a fop who went so far as to wear spats, and he walked with a waddle of his hips and spoke in a high-pitched feminine voice. We called him Miss Conway. He had been a server before Fisky and I came on the scene and claimed the right to be right-hand server, but we argued him out of this right—and the Rector backed us up. Furious and wriggling, he used to have to content himself with being a torch-bearer. He would sulk his way through the service, and afterwards toss his head at us before mincing his way out of the vestry to go home.

At mid-day, after lunch on Sunday—that is after sung Eucharist—the custom was that Fisky came round to our place, and the two of us sat under the porch and read Nelson Lees. But first we had a ritual to perform. The ritual of the Nut Pyramids.

Fisky arrived with the three or four brown-paper cones filled with peanuts (bought from Mother Chung's in St. Ann's Street). As he dismounted at the gateway he gave his own patented whistle, and I would whistle back in acknowledgment. Then while he was wheeling his Armstrong bike into the yard and under the portico, I went off to the kitchen, got the small metal mortar and pestle and ran downstairs and joined him, both of us sitting on a beam that connected two posts. We shelled the peanuts, put them into the mortar, and added sugar (which I had also fetched while getting the mortar and pestle from the kitchen). Then the pounding began. We took it in turns to pound, and when the nuts and sugar had been converted into an oily paste we took the whole mass out, built it into two pyramids, and then settled down to the pleasurable business of eating them. Then, and only then, did we lean back, each against his post, and fading out, faded in to the world of St. Frank's, or of Sexton Blake and Tinker on the trail of Doctor Huxton Rhymer, Professor Kew or Zenith the Albino.

Perhaps—an hour or two later—before he left, he would suddenly exclaim: "Wait! Didn't you get some new approval sheets from Errington and Martin!" And I would reply: "Yes. They came on Thursday by the *Biskra*. You want to see them?" And off I dashed upstairs to get the approval sheets.

The next half-hour would be filled with ecstatic sighs, whistlings and comments roughly as follows:

"Ph-ph-ew! Look at that Mozambique!"

"Spiffing, eh?"

"Oh, whoops! This is *just* the Sarawak I want to make up my set! Are you taking this, Barno?"

"No, I've got it already."

"Oh, good. I'll take it, then."

"Not the two Nyasalands next to it, though. I want those."

"I've got the one with the giraffe already. Unused, besides."

"Have you seen the new Ubangi-Shari set Linquvist sent me?"

"The chap in Denmark? Oooh! But look at *this*! A whole set of Seychelles!"

"Crown C A watermark."

"Not Script C A?"

"No. Crown C A. The old watermark. They're more valuable."

Chapter Nineteen

LESSONS AND WAR GAMES

FROM THE moment the new term began on the first of February, 1926, my way of life had to change—or, at least, appear to change. The Authorities had issued an edict . . . "You're taking the Junior Cambridge Examination in July. For the next few months you have to give all your attention to your lessons. So put away your stamp-album and your Nelson Lees until after July. Remember, you can't get into the Government Service unless you have a Junior Cambridge Certificate . . ." *Und so weiter* . . .

There was no real necessity, however, to caution me, for I was quite keen on taking the examination. The thought of my going into the Civil Service left me absolutely cold, but the challenge of an examination was exciting. Moreover, towards the end of the previous term a new headmaster had arrived to take the place of Old Rats, and he was a man we all admired and wanted to work for. He was the Reverend Mr. James Scrimgeour, a slim, taut man with a narrow face, thin-lipped and blue-green-eyed. He never caned. He had no need to. His eyes and his voice were enough. When he stared at you in rebuke his eyes emitted an icy fire shrivelling in its effect, and no leather could sting like the timbre of his voice loaded with the most delicately distilled sulphuric acid of sarcasm. He was a power-house of vitality. Every word he uttered registered, for there was the force of a strong will behind it. In his classes we never wanted to skylark because we were too engrossed in listening to him. He made everything interesting. Often he paused to illustrate some point with a crisp anecdote—always very crisp and very brief—but he never lost the trend of what he was talking about. He had a perfect sense of form. He never sat down, but moved about the room as he spoke in quick, controlled bursts of activity, halting abruptly at the blackboard to scribble something in relation to the subject under discussion, darting round, snapping his fingers as something else occurred to him. Brief anecdote . . . "Did you see in your newspaper recently what happened in Italy . . ?" And back to the subject.

The fee of entrance for the examination was $8.68 (British Guiana currency) which, at four shillings and two pence to the dollar, was equivalent to £1 16s. 2d. My term's fees had just been paid—$9.00—and it was a serious matter to have to pay, on top of this, $8.68 for the examination in July. The ugly spectre of impecuniousness, never absent in the gloom of the rafters, manifested itself with renewed vigour, poisoning the atmosphere with sighs and groans of frustration and depression. But once again it was the Rector who solved the problem. The Douglas Fund was still paying my regular school fees, so why not the fee for the examination, too?

The swotting began. And private lessons with Miss Glasgow.

The cost of these extra lessons was borne by the Authorities. I can't remember the amount involved, but I am sure it must have strained the supports of the forever frail budget structure. It is even possible that it meant sending a piece of jewellery to one of the Portuguese-run establishments that carried the sign of the three golden balls. It would not have been the first time that my mother had had recourse to do this. She herself, naturally, would rather have expired than been seen entering such a place, so she employed the services of one or other of the trusted ex-servants with whom she had kept up contact—one-time nannies or ex-cooks or ex-housemaids who had married and made homes of their own.

Miss Doris Glasgow was a mistress at the Girls' High School. Young, very brainy, and distinctly attractive, she had a shiveringly exciting laugh in which teeth, eyes and slim body joined, one factor alone sufficient to make lessons pleasant for Fisky and myself. But to increase the interest, she was also coaching Clara R—— who was Fisky's current casual heart-throb. (Though a year or two younger than I, he took his infatuations with the casualness of a happy extravert, unlike myself who took them with much mystery, brooding and interior sighing).

Miss Glasgow boarded with my aunt in Queenstown.

Uncle Henry Jones and Aunt Elfreda and family lived in a two-storied house with a perfect view of the river. In fact, it stood just opposite the spot where, in the eighteenth century and the early nineteenth century, a ferry operated. The guests of Governor van Batenburg landed here and made their way to Colony House, which still stands two hundred yards south along the road in what is now the Promenade Garden.

On Wednesday afternoons, after regular school, and on Saturday mornings Fisky and I made our way to Queenstown—often he towed me on his bike, or I towed him—and we discussed the usual topics: stamps, Nelson Lees and Sexton Blakes, which we still furtively read, girls and school politics. We might even have had a word to say about Freemasonry, for just opposite to my aunt's place, at the corner of Ferry Street, stood the Ituni (Freemasons') Lodge, and both our fathers were Freemasons. The dentist went to the meetings held on the first Monday in every month, but my own father went only occasionally, when invited, because he could not afford to pay the annual subscription. He kept his apron in a small black leather brief-case, and once or twice, very reluctantly, he showed it to me, doing it as if it might have been some secret object of international importance entrusted to his care by Sexton Blake.

Sometimes, after lessons with Miss Glasgow, we would ask permission of my aunt to roam around the grounds—about three acres—and help ourselves to whatever fruit we could find that was ripe enough to be picked. If it was a wet day, it might mean having to endure the bites of the mosquitoes, but to anyone who had grown up in New Amsterdam, this was treated as an accepted inconvenience, like a sand-storm to a Bedouin in the Sahara, or a November fog to a Londoner. Every seasoned New Amsterdamer knows that with the rains come the mosquitoes, with the dry season—sand-flies at dusk.

On one occasion we managed to persuade Uncle Henry to show us his stamp collection. We had heard about it but never seen it. It turned out to be a rather haphazard affair, but it contained some excellent specimens of early British Guiana issues. The 1860 set evoked a lot of "Whoops!" and "Ooops!" and expressive whistles. The 1897 Jubilees did more than this. They made us lean forward with hungry, predatory, gaping mouths. They were not arranged in complete set-order, starting from the lowest value and ending with the highest, but were simply stuck in at random—and we noticed that there were a number of *duplicates*! And unused! Unable to restrain myself, I pounced . . . "Uncle Henry, I think that's another fifteen-cent Jubilee there . . ." And Uncle Henry, in his bland, brisk, hypocritical way, started and stared at the stamp I was pointing at, as though astounded, incredulous. Was it possible that there actually was a duplicate! . . . He gave a hesitant chuckle . . . "Yes. So it is! Huh-huh!" . . . "Could I have it, Uncle Henry?" He frowned, uttered another hesitant chuckle, and said: "Let's see. I think there's another one somewhere else." And he began to turn frantically—until . . . "Yes, yes. Here we are!" It was another fifteen-cent Jubilee. But it had a cockroach stain in the bottom right-hand corner. Smiling and triumphant, full of generosity, he jerked it out of the album and handed it over . . . Not a minute later, Fisky pounced . . . "Look! A five-cent! It's a duplicate! Can I have it?" Once again, the astounded, incredulous start . . . "Ah . . . Let's see. I'm sure . . ." A swift flick-flick, and . . . "Yes, yes! Here we are. You can have this one, my boy." He jerked it out and presented it to Fisky with a nod and a smile. Another cockroach stain—in the upper left-hand corner.

Despite the furious swotting for the examination, I still found time to read *The Times* war-books. I could read these openly on Saturdays and Sundays at home, without any protest from the Authorities. For some reason, no one thought they would distract me from my studies. They did not—but they took possession of my imagination to such an extent that I was not satisfied merely to play war games with paper pellets in class; I sat down and thought up a game that could be played on a board.

With the examination hardly a month away, I cut out an oblong piece of cardboard and sketched out a battlefield array of opposing trenches and forts. At the one end of the board the Germans were solidly massed in two or three lines that stretched across the entire Sector. The rest of the board consisted of French villages and forts scattered haphazardly here and there and linked together by roads. I manufactured my own counters. They took the form, in the case of the Germans, of bits of the soft silvery (was it lead?) wrapping out of which tea-packets were made in those days. Each bit was folded into a solid, tiny blob that could fit into one of the squares of space into which the "roads" were divided. For the French I dropped little blobs of sealing-wax on to a plate and let them set, then collected the whole lot and put them into a matchbox. The Germans were outnumbered by the French in the ratio of about two to three, but they were more firmly entrenched and less vulnerable. The French, scattered about in various villages and forts and Hills, were always in danger of being wiped out, one by one, in swift German thrusts. The general idea of the game was to throw dice and move the men in accordance with the amount that turned up. The first to break through into the rearmost of the other's lines won the game. A break-through meant that you had to get twelve men into the rearmost line.

According to my diary, I made this game on the third of June. I introduced it to Fisky and Eric Cossou on the following day, and it was an immediate success. They were both very keen. The very next day, a Saturday, news came to Coburg Street that Fisky had met with an accident near a canal at Plantation Providence, about two miles out of town. He had stepped on to a long, rusty nail after a swim in the canal, and had to be taken to hospital. I went to see him in the late afternoon—and I took the war-game. It was just what he wanted, and we played game after game until it was time for me to leave. He had to remain in hospital for about two weeks, and at least four times a week I went to see him, taking the game. Other chaps sometimes accompanied me, and joined the fun. We played tournaments, and the results were generally close, for the two sides were about evenly matched, despite the seemingly solid and unbroken lines of the Germans at the one end of the board. On three successive days, the scores read as follows: 5–5; 6–5, in favour of Eric; 6–4, in my favour. On the 22nd, I note: "Went to see John à l'hôpital. Played War Game. French men mown down (8–8)." On the 24th, I went to the hospital, but found that John was not in the ward. However, I "met him and towed him home. Played War Game with him. (9–9)."

Chapter Twenty

TEENAGER IN THE 'TWENTIES

TO BE A TEENAGER in the nineteen-twenties was, I suppose, as interesting as to be a teenager in the latter half of the 'forties. Both were post-war, transition periods. Clothes have never interested me, but even I could not fail to notice the change in women's fashions: the withering away of corsets and the shortening skirts, the nightgown-dresses that were sometimes revealingly transparent, excitingly so when there was anything underneath worthwhile revealing, to wit: the wife of an elder brother of one of the boys at school when she made her entrance at a prize-day ceremony; I still remember the gasp I gave, and how I clasped my hands and blinked. The bobbed hair, at first ridiculous, soon became so commonplace that one wondered if long hair ever had been the fashion.

The most sensational changes, from my point of view, were in the ballroom—or perhaps the drawing-room would be a better word, for it was in drawing-rooms that dances were held. Though not yet old enough to dance, my sister and I were often permitted to accompany our mother and aunts to an evening function at some home where there might be casual dancing to the music of a piano and violin. Sometimes we were even allowed to accompany them to "Rosedale" to a straightforward dance. Thus we were able to watch lancers and the waltz gradually give way to the quick-step and the one-step and fox-trot, and then stare and giggle at the absurdities of the Charleston. Ragtime music, as I had heard it called, had seemed silly enough, but the first wailings of the saxophone struck me as both weird and silly. (Even to this day in 1961 I am baffled how anyone could listen to jazz in a mood of seriousness). Though I had not yet been introduced to the music of Wagner, which has held me entranced from the middle 'thirties, I could still discern the tinsel, tissue quality of jazz. Later it entertained me—I danced to it with much enjoyment, even treasured certain tunes for their sentimental associations—but it never impressed me as music meant for being listened to.

The gaiety of the 'twenties made itself felt even in remote little New Amsterdam. Concerts of a serious kind—generally given by Aunt Lou in her own home or in the Town Hall; she played the mandolin, Uncle Bertie played the violin, and sopranos and tenors and baritones sang solos—continued to flourish, but a new kind came into being—the concert at which people engaged in music-hall turns, and sang the popular jazz songs. Once I myself took part in one which Mr. Muss arranged in aid of our Scout troop; I think it was in order to raise funds for our new club-room. With about three other chaps I had to sing Irving Berlin's *What'll I do?* on the Town Hall stage. Eric Cossou's uncle did a comic turn with an attractive girl, in the course of which they sang *When it's night-time in Italy it's Wednesday over here.*

The Berbice Musical Society, in which the Reverend Mr. Cossou, Eric's father, and my Aunt Anna took an active part, periodically put on shows of one kind or another; sometimes it was the popular music-hall stuff and sometimes it was Gilbert and Sullivan—*The Gondoliers* or *The Mikado*, *The Pirates of Penzance* or *Trial by Jury*. (Shortly after I left school I took part in an operetta called *The Mandarin*). It was Aunt Anna who made me aware of the beauty in music. I had given up learning to play the piano after getting as far as the duet stage in Hemy's; it had meant no more to me then than a dreary round of "exercises", monotonously played every morning, starting from the most elementary five-finger chores right through the scales and the potted tunes to the half-page études, Concert Marches and Characteristic Airs, near the middle of the book. I used to dash through the whole mess at such an impatient speed, striking so many wrong notes and putting such *expression* into my playing (boiling, scowling anger) that the Authorities decided that I had better stop. But when I dropped in at "Rosedale" Aunt Anna, a widow—Mrs. McLean—would encourage me to sit with her at the piano while she played me excerpts from various operas and operettas, and sometimes even bits of Schubert and Chopin and Beethoven. And she told me about the music as she played. She explained what it was all about, put meaning and substance into it, gave it a significance for me that formerly it had not had. She was an unusual person. So different from her elder sisters, in physical appearance and in temperament, that I am inclined to believe the many rumours I have heard that she was not a Mittelholzer. The story goes—and the evidence is very strong—that my paternal grandmother, in her latter years, was guilty of a certain amount of naughtiness, either in or out of the manse, and the gentleman implicated was a well-known business man, very dark in complexion and with kinky hair: a Mr. George G——. It is certainly odd that Aunt Anna was the only child with kinky hair *and* an olive complexion *and* features of a distinctly negroid cast. And it was odd, too, that Mr. George G— should have taken an almost proprietary interest in her from childhood until she was a young woman, as many people have testified. After marrying, she spent some time in Scotland with her husband, and it was on her return to the colony, and after his death, that she became caught up in amateur theatricals and music, and eventually arrived in New Amsterdam to live at ''Rosedale''. She had an independent, uninhibited approach to every situation, and detested stuffiness of any variety. She did not hesitate to take a job in one of the cinemas playing the piano for the silent films.

In Coburg Street, Ethel M. Dell and Ruby M. Ayres had begun to displace Hall Caine and Marie Corelli in popularity. *The Way of an Eagle* took the place of Mrs. Henry Wood's *East Lynne* as a work of genius in the estimation of my mother and aunts. E. M. Hull (*The Sheik*) and Elinor Glyn (*Three Weeks*) were the D. H. Lawrences to be enjoyed in guilty secrecy and with many muffled exclamations of scandalized delight.

Pearson's Weekly was still Dad's favourite periodical, but *Pearson's Magazine* as well as *The Strand Magazine* sometimes featured on his lap-board in the morning before breakfast, provided that he was not using the lap-board for sketching something—or for working on an illuminated address. One after the other he turned out these addresses; it had become a fixed fashion in the colony after the occasion in 1919 when he had done the one for the Prince of Wales. A new Governor arrived, so the Municipicality of Georgetown or of New Amsterdam had to give him a "civic" welcome in the Town Hall, so they wrote and asked Dad to execute an address of welcome. The head of a big firm was retiring, so the office-staff decided that he must be given an address along with a parting gift, so they approached Dad and gave him the commission. These welcoming and retiring occasions occurred, on an average, a dozen times a year; sometimes he found himself with two or three on his hands at the same time. He never liked refusing, because it meant additional income. Even for those times, his salary as Town Accountant (equivalent to Assistant Town Clerk) was shamefully small. It caused him a lot of bitterness when, on more than one occasion, he was passed over for promotion. Considering the meticulous care he put into his work and the extra time he gave to it, he felt that when, as happened twice, the post of Town Clerk became vacant, he ought automatically to have been appointed. But no. Even after he had acted for six or seven months as Town Clerk, the Council decided to get an outsider to fill the post. Several factors counted against my father. The first was his unsociable disposition; he never mixed with the Councillors, even though he had gone to school with many of them and was acquainted with them. Mr. Luckhoo, when he was Mayor, often asked him over for a drink and a chat, but Dad always made an excuse; he was not a drinker, and he was not fond of conversation; he liked his routine and his own company. Secondly, his shyness and retiring nature were felt by the Councillors to be qualities not fitting for a Town Clerk. They wanted a man with "personality". Something else that probably counted against him—though I never heard it clearly expressed—was his appearance. He simply could not be persuaded to pay attention to his clothes; a suit would grow shabbier and shabbier, but he seemed completely unaware of the fact. He wore a straw hat—a boater—and when it got yellow or stained from long wear, he would paint it with enamel—an off-white tint—and continue to wear it, despite the protests of my mother that it looked ridiculous.

It was in the 'twenties that the Lutheran Church became completely Americanised. It was financed by the Lutheran Church in America, and they sent their own pastors. In our home, my grandmother, the one-time Congregationalist, had, some years before, joined the Lutheran Church, and so she was the only one who attended the noon-day or evening services—that is, when it was convenient for her to be taken to church, for her crippled condition made going to church an irregular business. When the Pastor came to our home he came to see her—not the Mittelholzers: those renegades to Anglo-Catholicism. Not to my aunts, who were also Anglicans. But, as I have remarked somewhere before, the Sunday School was a different matter. My sister and I attended the Lutheran Sunday School, which was rated the best in the town. The Pastor saw to it that everything was done to "boost" the membership. Attractive tracts were distributed every week, and a scheme was instituted to encourage regular attendance. You were given a bronze medal if you attended regularly for a certain number of successive Sundays, and then a silver for a further period—and then a gold. And there were other "buttons" and medals to be won if you introduced new members. Fierce competition arose between teachers to win the button or medal for the best run class, and the hunger for glory of one sort or another grew from week to week among both pupils and teachers. Something sensational was perpetually in the air. If it were not a Pageant, it was a big do to commemorate the first or second anniversary of the Pastor's pastorship, or the inauguration of the new organ. Once it was the ceremony of the unveiling of a stained glass window in memory of Pastor John Robert Mittelholzer. I had to sit in a front pew with Dad and my sister and other members of the clan while Sir Edward Davson uttered appropriate words, and Lady Davson graciously performed the actual unveiling.

Meanwhile, the Rector of All Saints, now a Canon, continued on his High Church course, adding new touches of colour and pageantry to the ritual. We sacristans discarded our purple cassocks in favour of virgin-white albs. Processions became more elaborate and more frequent. And the Canon was a musician. He himself coached the choir on Thursday evenings, and sung Eucharist was treated at Easter and Whitsuntide and at Christmas as a major musical occasion. Sometimes, at the altar, the Canon would turn and hiss and gesture at the altos or the basses when they went wrong. Once, during an Easter procession, when the grand *Hail, Festal Day* was being sung, I made the mistake of continuing to sing when only the bass cantors had to be doing so, and the Canon touched me quickly and uttered an urgent: "Sssh!" I was cope-bearing.

Chapter Twenty-one

IDYLL AND WARRIOR

TWO ELEMENTS have always lived within me, side by side and in restless harmony, something, no doubt, after the fashion of uranium atoms. Any positive disturbance, and the precarious symbiosis dissolved into roaring chaos. The Idyll Element dreamed of a peaceful, sylvan situation ("a Book of Verse—and Thou beside me") and life proceeding with oiled precision, secure under cosy, twilit rafters, with rain, thunder and lightning, sunshine and the rustling of trees providing a simple, satisfying variety in the flow of the days and the weeks and months, even the years. The Warrior Element listened always to the sound of the Conflict, was perpetually alert to the raw actuality of Life, perpetually ready to resist, to repulse, to do battle to the death with any foe that might appear. *Greensleeves* weaving through the Sword motiv from *The Ring*.

Outside of school, J.P. and I haunted each other (I soon stopped calling him Fisky). Apart from our Sunday after-lunch date for Nelson Lees and the Nut Pyramids, we sometimes went for long strolls after Evensong and jawed about everything that interested us. Why we became such close friends is one of those mysteries of human nature, for though our interests were similar—stamp-collecting and reading—our attitudes and our temperaments were at complete variance. I brooded on things, took a serious view of everything I indulged in, whether it was my stamp-collecting, or writing to the Amalgamated Press or Mr. E. S. Brooks, whether altar-serving or the girl who had currently become Number One in my devotion. J.P. never brooded on anything—at least, not so that it showed up in his behaviour. He laughed everything off in a casual, carefree fashion. He would never have dreamt of sending subscriptions to the Amalgamated Press or writing to the author of the Nelson Lee stories; too much bother; he left such spade-work to me. And as for girls, he treated them as though he were a sultan who could pluck from a richly stocked harem whatever luscious items he required and whenever he required. One, his attitude implied, ought never to get flustered about one's little feminine fun. We met at one point—the satirical. We were both mockers. In a crowd, we liked horse-play and clowning and jeering. In our own company, we mocked each other, but lightly and with some caution. We argued sometimes and even disagreed about this and that, yet, somehow, the trembling balance between the Idyll Element and the Warrior Element never shifted enough to cause me to explode. In company, however, a minor flare-up could happen, chiefly because J.P.'s weak spot was his vanity; you had to be careful not to drop any dark comments directed against his home or family. Unlike with me, his background was something sacred. I would even have encouraged adverse comments on Coburg Street, but, to him, "Westbourne Villa" politics were taboo in company. His father was renowned as the best dentist not only in the town but in the colony, and to compliment him was in order; to hurl the smallest pebble of criticism was to wound his son into swift anger. J.P.'s vanity was a clan-vanity.

In school, he shared a desk with another boy. I shared one with Eric Cossou, but with Eric I could be close only on the level of horse-play. We jabbered banalities, teased the girls who came over to join us for certain subjects, manufactured paper ammunition for bombarding Positions in our class-room war, carved our initials on desks and posts, and generally tried to outdo each other in clowning of one sort or another. I could never thresh out the subtleties of any subject or situation with him as I could with J.P. We lived for class-room moments. Out of school, we met for games or to exchange Nelson Lees and Sexton Blakes. And sometimes he towed me home on his bicycle. Whatever explosions occurred in me because of my contacts with him were squib-like and superficial.

It was at home that the major detonations took place, because it was at home that Actuality assaulted me. It was at home that my masculinity was perpetually under attack. My mother never lost the desire to inflict corporal punishment on me even when I was in my teens. The last time she went for me with Tickle Toby was one day when I was well over fourteen—and after that she threatened but never again wielded the leather with any effect. The Warrior flamed in me, and I grabbed Tickle Toby and yanked it away from her. How I restrained myself from attacking her and striking her still baffles me, for I trembled with a tiger-like fury. She recoiled, and it was probably this that saved her. I saw the fear on her face, mingled with her own fury.

It was different, however, one day on the playing-field at school. During Recess, we were supposed to do P.T. This was a new institution, and a new master, a square, hulking Canadian called Pachal, had been assigned to put us through our paces. We went racing into the playing-field, frolicking and fractious and intractable, and Mr. Pachal kept waving, and bawling at us to get into line. One or two docile souls fell into line, but confirmed roysterers like myself paid no attention. I continued to gallop about the field . . . "Mittelholzer! Get into line!" But Mittelholzer went on chasing Cyril Chu, yelling and reaching out a grabbing hand . . . Suddenly behind me came a quick thump-thump of foot-treads, and something grasped the back of my coat while a knee collided with my buttocks. I turned, and saw the angry face of Pachal. Explosion! My mind instantly registered the fact that I had been kicked, and the Warrior went into action. I slammed an upper-cut into Pachal's jaw, and raised my fists, waiting for him to come at me. He was too shocked to renew the assault. He stared at me—and with trembling head, I launched out on a flaming verbal attack. He backed away, ordering me to get into the school and wait there. I told him to go to hell, and refused to move. I challenged him to fight. He stammered out something incoherent, again ordered me off the field. Again I refused. The other boys stood around in a rigid, staring circle. I shouted at him like a mad man. Eventually, it was he who had to leave the field. He went off to report me to the Headmaster.

I was suspended until the incident was investigated. Long before I got home they had heard. It was all over the town, apparently, in less than an hour. They backed me at home . . . "What! He actually raised his *foot* to you!" For once, my father was forced to take a hand in my affairs. I cannot remember if it was the Headmaster he saw, but there was some meeting between him and one or other of the masters, and Pachal apologised for his hasty action. The Headmaster said that the whole incident was a regrettable one on both sides and decided to let it be forgotten. I was allowed to return to school.

Henceforth, Pachal and I were the best of friends. Once or twice he would even let me take charge of the class in French (which was my strongest subject) while he went off to prepare an experiment in the science laboratory (science was his strong subject). The Idyll Element in me, as swift and wholehearted in its welcome of peace as was the Warrior Element of war when the battle-trumpets sounded, took full charge of the situation.

Whether strong emotions were involved or not, any situation that contained the factor of conflict stimulated me, set a dynamo humming in me. When I was in the lower forms, the senior boys would sometimes throw out a challenge, daring any of the juniors to enter the Senior Room. At Recess, they would stand at the door of the Senior Room and threaten to hurl off any juniors who approached. This was just what I loved. I immediately organised an attacking force, and we threw ourselves at the enemy. The seniors resisted, struggling with us, but also laughing and treating the affair as a joke. Some of us would fight our way half-way into the room, then outside we went, swiftly and ignominiously propelled by three or four pairs of hands. Not with me, however, I always fought my way right to the farthest corner of the room and proclaimed myself the victor by standing on a desk and shouting it out. I took it seriously, and squirmed out of the clutching hands, dodged, and charged everything in my path, for the one object remained fixed in my will. I *had* to reach the goal agreed on as the point of victory. Had the enemy taken it in the same determined spirit they could easily have hurled me out every time, I am certain.

In our Scout troop, we sometimes played a game called cock-fighting. You had to hop around, holding one ankle behind, while you charged at your opponent in an attempt to make him lose his balance and thus force him to release his ankle and stand on both feet. I used to take on the whole troop, one boy after the other, and emerge the victor. It could have been that I had exceptionally good balance, but I am inclined to think that the real reason for my defeating every member of the troop was that I willed myself *not* to go down. It was a struggle, and I never treated a struggle lightly.

The same went for table-tennis. I could never smash—and to this day I cannot—but I always played a stolidly defensive game, patiently and carefully returning everything that came over to me, until my opponent, enraged at the never-ending rally, did something drastic and sent the ball wide or into the net. I did not always win, but those who eventually got the better of me did so only after a long and harrowing struggle.

For cricket I could not build up any kind of enthusiasm. I found it too slow and laborious—that is, however, when it was played according to the rules. In the back-yard at "Westbourne Villa", we played a rough-and-ready version in which the idea was that the fielders competed among themselves to win a spell of batting. If you managed to grab the ball when the batsman swiped it, or if it missed the wicket and you were at long stop, or even wicket-keeper, you became bowler and sent down a scorcher. If somebody else caught the batsman out, however, he it was who went in to bat, not you the bowler. It was a purely cut-throat business. I enjoyed this kind of cricket immensely. It was exciting and highly competitive. We all enjoyed it—until the ball crashed through a window and ended up on the floor of the dentist's surgery. That generally brought the afternoon's play to an abrupt conclusion.

Soccer fascinated me. Here was continuous action; fast, rugged conflict. I threw all my zest into it, and eventually won a place in the school team—at right-half. But, sad to relate, I was no good. I was a hopeless failure. No amount of persistence made the slightest difference. Whenever I tried to kick a ball it went off at an angle of about sixty degrees of the intended direction. That is when I did succeed in kicking it. Three times out of four I mis-kicked. The team-captain assured me quite frankly that he played me in the team only because I was a good worrier. No forward could ever hope to get through our defence without encountering a stubborn harrying from me, provided he was on the opponents' left-wing, of course. True, the ball might go over the touch-line more often than it would be wrested away by me and fed to my own forward line, but I invariably succeeded in upsetting the schemes of the other side's left-wingers.

If it was to be defeat, the Warrior must go down fighting. A tame retreat, a tame surrender, was unthinkable!

Chapter Twenty-two

LONG TROUSERS

THE FATEFUL Junior Cambridge Examination went off without hitch. My diary records: "Did Object Drawing and Gospel. Did well in both." And on the following day, 14th July: "Went to Exam. Geometry, Dictation and The Acts. Did well in all." Which, I am certain, was an instance of faulty reporting. I detested Geometry in the upper forms, and hardly bothered to pretend to take an interest in it. The same went for Algebra. I had no flair for mathematics, though I liked Arithmetic which, to me, was merely a matter of simple logic; commonsense juxtaposing of a few given factors followed by addition, subtraction, multiplication and division: you just had to be careful to see that you did your additions, subtractions, etc. without making any silly slips. It was a good thing that I did like Arithmetic, because, in this examination, it was, with Dictation, a Compulsory. If you failed in Arithmetic and Dictation, you could get credits in all the other subjects—but you failed the examination as a whole. Despite my comment in my diary, I did very badly in Geometry. On the 20th, I tackled the Algebra paper, but my diary makes no comment on my performance. Just as well. I did equally as badly as I did in Geometry.

It would be interesting to compare the notes in my diary on what I thought I had done in each subject with the results that appeared in November. In Object Drawing and Gospel, I secured passes—just ordinary P. In Geometry I got a B—bad failure. I passed in Dictation, though evidently it was not the custom to publish any detailed mark-symbol for this subject. For The Acts I scored an M 3—which meant I had got a credit and had been placed third in the group entered for our school. In Algebra I did a little better than in Geometry—

I got an F. Failure but not a *bad* failure! My diary states that I "did well" in *As You Like It* and *Kenilworth*, two separate subjects. I even added: "Ate up." But in November the examiners reported that I failed in Shakespeare and got an M 2 for Scott. I "did well in both Flat Drawing and Hygiene. Hygiene easy." Results: A pass in Flat Drawing, and I was the only one to get an M in Hygiene. "Arithmetic and French. All right in former. Did well in latter. Ate up." I passed in Arithmetic (no credit) and got an M in French—the only one to get an M in that Subject. On the 21st of July it was "rainy. Went in car. History and Memory Drawing and English Grammar. Ate up 2 former." Why I should have specified the "two former" and left out English Grammar I have no idea, for the examiners gave me a G 1 in English Grammar, an M 1 in History and a G 1 in Memory Drawing. I topped our group in all three, and with credits, to boot. In the examination, as a whole, I came second in merit, and, of course, having passed in Arithmetic and Dictation, I had *passed*!

The concentrated effort of preparing for the examination had caused me to neglect my Nelson Lees and Sexton Blakes which, meanwhile, had been piling up in my drawer. But on the very evening of the last day of the examination I pounced on the pile and began to read. And there was such a back-log of reading to catch up on that during the holiday weeks that followed I broke my custom and did not write a long story in a fat exercise book. The year before I had written *The Secret of the Ring*. However, in the middle of the new term, on the 31st of October, a Sunday evening, I "started to write story". And all through November I was busy on it, despite school work. On the 18th I "wrote Chap. 7 *Caves of Kaieteur*." I finished it on the 22nd. One of the boys who sat behind me in class, Frankie de Mendonça, heard me talking about it, and when I was about two-thirds way through the story, I let him read it in instalments; it filled about four exercise books. Frankie was so enthusiastic about it and seemed so keen to see "next week's exciting instalment" that other boys asked to read it, too. Flattered, I was only too pleased to oblige.

No one stopped me from indulging my favourite occupation.

Everyone was too satisfied at the results of the examination. That Christmas was an exceptionally enjoyable one. As was the custom, we went shopping on Christmas Eve night, though almost all the shopping that had to be done had already been achieved during the week before. But most important of all—for me—was the head-spinning, head-swelling event to which all boys at that time looked forward. I went into long trousers!

Yes. Previously I had worn shorts, because I was deemed a "mere boy". But suddenly I had become a big boy. My height, on the 13th of November, was five feet nine (weight, eight stone, six). I was tall enough to wear longs. In fact, I had been tall enough a long time before (on the 10th of October, 1925, says my diary, I was five feet seven; weight: seven stone, twelve). But the Authorities did not take such statistics into consideration. A boy was as old as his *age*. Had I been twelve feet tall I would probably have been kept in shorts until I had reached the age of seventeen!

I bought a roll of film, and J.P. came and took several pictures of me wearing my longs. Shortly the roll would be developed, and one or two prints would be sent off to Grandfather David Leblanc, who still lived in retirement in Barbados, a bridge-playing gentleman of leisure. He wrote my father monthly when he sent the cheque for Grandma's maintenance. He never wrote to Grandma. Occasionally he wrote to Mother. He was very proud of his grandchildren—especially of his grandsons, for he had suffered a great disappointment when his only son died at the age of about four or five. Moreover, he had expressed great pleasure on hearing that I had passed my examination. Every year he sent us money for Christmas. This year he sent me nearly double what he usually sent.

When I went shopping on Christmas Eve night, very self-conscious in my long trousers, I was still the boy living in his Idyll Dream. The Warrior dozed. The familiar carols wove a cool peace in the humid air. Who wanted to think about 1927 and what might be waiting there? Rumours had already rumbled in the rafters concerning the alternatives of putting the boy into harness or letting him take the Senior School Certificate. But it was Christmas. Forget actuality. Tomorrow there would be Christmas dinner. Turnips-and-carrots soup. Cabbage. Turkey and chicken and ham. Dates. Walnuts. Almonds. And the boy was wearing long trousers. A five-foot-nine boy—as tall as many men of thirty, forty and fifty. He *looked* like a man, even if he still thought and behaved like a boy.

Yes. It was a good Christmas.

"Good day. Went to 5 a.m. Mass only. Had a good time all day. Beau temps. John came in day. Bought 80 cents stamps from E & M Appros. Had crackers at dinner in night. Good time."

Chapter Twenty-three

EXAMINATIONS AND FASCINATIONS

ALL THROUGH January the debate was fought. Dad was all for my looking for a job. He had not been concerned about my sitting for the Junior Cambridge, and now that I had passed this examination, he felt that it was enough. Why should I go on to win further scholastic laurels? At seventeen? "Time you went into harness!" Not that he really tried to enforce anything. He merely threw off his opinions in a casual manner when the topic was brought up. Not that he had any plans in view for me. He had talked to no one of his acquaintances with the idea of sounding out the prospects of a job for me. Nor did any of us expect him to take action of any sort. The debate, such as it was, was carried on between my mother and my aunts and grandmother, with myself sometimes consulted for reactions to this or that suggestion . . . "I think you ought to learn shorthand and typing." Reaction: "I don't mind." Further debate, then: "I think you ought to apply at once for a post in the Government." Reaction: "Now? But am I the right age yet?" Rebuttal: "You have to be eighteen, but your application would be put on file, and perhaps when you're eighteen they'll send for you." Reaction: "Oh, I see." Further debate, then: "Would you like to sit for the Senior School Certificate?" Reaction: "Yes, I'd like to!"

It was resolved, therefore, that I should take the School Certificate Examination in July, but with the understanding that, in the meantime, negotiations should begin in respect to the Government job.

A friend of the family—a Mr. T——; he boarded at "Rosedale"—was well established in the Civil Service. As Magistrate's Clerk, he was able to predict that a vacancy was soon to occur in the Magistrate's Office. A junior clerk was needed. This was just what Mother wanted to hear. She spoke to Mr. T—— and asked him if he would help me to secure this post. Of course he would. And to show his good intentions, he invited me to call at the Magistrate's Office one morning when no one but himself was present. The Magistrate often went into the country for sessions of the court held in various districts. I called, and he showed me what sort of work might be required of me if I got the post. I nearly fell asleep from boredom. He kept mumbling about "jackets" and depositions and documents tied in pink tape, and told me how a summons had to be made out. Then he put me on the typewriter to practise typing. He was very kind and patient, and it was no fault of his that the whole business was boring. I was simply not interested in legal procedures and officialdom. The typewriter interested me, and I rather liked to see the words appearing on the sheet of paper when I struck the keys—though the gadgets that controlled margins got me impatient.

Early in March I was made to write a letter of application to the Colonial Secretary in Georgetown. This was the official next in rank to the Governor, and it was his office that made appointments. Together with this letter I sent "recommendations" from the Rector and a Mr. S——, the office manager of S.D. & Co. who was a good friend of the Rector's and also casually acquainted with my father. I regarded the matter as drab and dull in the extreme, and certainly felt no excitement at the prospect of becoming a Civil Servant.

What interested me particularly during this period was the painting of landscape scenes or flowers in girls' autograph albums. It developed into a craze, and, as the word spread, more and more girls began to offer me their albums for contributions. At the same time I discovered among a roomful of old books at "Rosedale"—books that had belonged to my grandfather, the Lutheran pastor—a number of German grammars, and instantly I resolved to begin learning German. The German text did not dismay me. I soon mastered it, and the declensions as well which reminded me of Latin and did not seem in any way strange. In no time I had discovered that the plural of *Holz* was *Hölzer*, and a theory suggested itself to me. The Pastor must have been careless! Or he must have wanted to make a concession to his British nationality—hence the non-appearance of the Umlaut in our name. Very well. I would put the matter right. I would restore the Umlaut.

I began to spell our name Mittelhölzer. Dad noticed this, and when I explained, he approved. It certainly looked more German spelt this way. So straightway he adopted the new spelling. And so did my brothers very shortly afterwards. And later my sister. Not Mother. She was not a Germanophile.

It was not until 1951 when, in London, I was told by a Swiss journalist that the original members of my family in Switzerland did not use the Umlaut, that it occurred to me that the old pastor had been guilty of no carelessness, nor had he made any concessions to his British nationality. So I dropped the Umlaut as abruptly as I had adopted it.

Soccer continued to fascinate me. I turned up for practice as often as I could, and whenever a match of any importance between the big teams in the town was played on the Parade Ground I was on the scene to back the team of my choice—and to cadge for the honour of running lines. The two giants were the Crystal Palace and the Casuals. The former was composed entirely of black boys and youngish men, the latter of olive-complexioned chaps of the middle-class. I backed the Casuals as a matter of form, and even entertained the hope of one day being able to play for them. Frankie de Mendonça, one of my form-mates, was their inside-right—though he also played for our school team.

The reading of Nelson Lees and Sexton Blakes was suspended—purely as a gesture to impress the Authorities. Stamp-collecting activities, which, for some reason, were not frowned upon, continued as usual; in fact, they may even be said to have intensified, because I had started a fierce correspondence with other stamp-collectors all over the world—Canada, Australia, New Zealand, South Africa, France and England being the countries most strongly featured.

The weather has always fascinated me—far more than soccer, which proved a mere passing phase, and equally as much as stamp-collecting and Nelson Lees. My enthusiasm for recording the state of the weather never flagged throughout all the time I have kept a diary. It was at this period that, encouraged by what I had learnt in science class at school, I made a rain-gauge and set it up in the back-yard. I already had an alcohol thermometer (obtained free, because it advertised a well-known brand of Dutch gin), but now I took it into my head that I ought to possess one with a mercury column. So I bought some quicksilver, and made something that *passed* for a thermometer; it would be absurd to call it one. It consisted of a plain piece of window-pane glass cut down to about six inches by three on to which I pasted a piece of paper, leaving down the middle a thin hollow space. It was down this hollow space that I forced a small quantity of mercury; at the bottom of the space I had allowed enough room to create a "bulb", and it was out of this larger area that the column rose. I took the whole contraption to school and "graded" it, using the thermometer in the science laboratory as a guide. The astounding thing is that it did work—for about two or three days. After that the "bulb" began to spread out like an island on a map as the gum on the paper yielded to the moisture in the air; the column dropped, and the whole grading became automatically worthless; what was eighty degrees the day before now registered as seventy-two, or even sixty-eight. And when I put it against my chest blood temperature was no longer ninety-eight, but eighty or seventy-eight.

The rain-gauge was not treated as recommended by the best authorities. Had I set it up in an open space on the ground—like the one in the Promenade Garden—there is no saying how many stray dogs would have contributed to the amount of rain collected. So what I did was to sling it out in mid-air, suspended between bedroom and shaddock tree. I arranged my strings in such a way that I could pull it in to the window every morning, or after any very heavy shower, and take the Reading. I always had a high old time with this gauge, for in British Guiana the average annual rainfall is 100 inches. One good brisk shower can amount to nearly an inch. In the periods of the year when the rains are very heavy, it is nothing for two or three inches to fall in as many hours. Thus, in my diary, I record: "Rained heavily in early morning. 2.27 ins." And the following day: "Very rainy in afternoon. 2.43 ins. fell." My younger brothers, who, at this time, were inclined to imitate me in most things, were quite delighted with the idea of a rain-gauge suspended between house and tree, so straightway each of them made gauges of their own. After a night of heavy rain, it was a stimulating sight, the three of us hauling in our gauges to see how many inches had collected!

Meantime, I was in no way neglecting my lessons. The same old pattern of late-evening studying repeated itself. But I did not take any private lessons with anybody. The Authorities probably felt that I could be trusted to work on my own in conjunction with the help from the masters at school. There was much head-shaking among the boys of the upper-school, however, at my contemptuous attitude towards Maths. For the situation was this: to pass the School Certificate you had to do well in Geometry and Algebra *and* English or History. If you failed in Geometry and Algebra and passed very well (that is, got credits) in Geography and Arithmetic, that would be considered satisfactory, *provided* you also passed in the English or History Section. Things, in those days, were made as tricky as possible. However, I was exceptionally good in Geography, and I was putting my trust in that subject, and also trusting that I would be able to get a credit in Arithmetic. I knew it was hopeless trying to do anything with Geometry and Algebra. It would simply be time wasted if I attempted to master these, so I just left them alone entirely, even though I had automatically registered for them in my application.

I did not suffer from examination nerves, and, in July, sat down with confidence to tackle the papers put before me. On the first day, we had Hygiene, English Composition and Geography. I mopped them all up. The other chaps groaned when they related what they had done in Geography. Contours, isotherms and isobars, had all featured in the first part: Physical Geography. But I was smiling. "I ate it up," I told them. "Elementary!" . . . "And what subject did you choose in Composition?" they asked. "The Earth's Crust," I told them. "But I didn't do it as an essay. I did it as a short story." Which was what I had done. I ignored the fact that the examiners had asked me to write an essay. Enthusiastic as I was about everything geographical, I decided that a subject like The Earth's Crust was just the thing for me to let my imagination loose upon. I did not even stop to ponder on the significance of the word "crust". Had I done so I would have realised that it carried more a geological than a geographical connotation. Anyway, I bent over my desk and let my imagination take charge. I wrote a short story describing the adventures of a man travelling across South America, from the Andes to Buenos Aires (complete with racy dialogue), and after an exciting time in mountain and forest and Patagonian desert, our hero arrived safely in the Argentine capital, and I ended my story with the observation: "How varied is the Earth's crust!"

The following day, I got through all the problems in Arithmetic, but was not certain whether my final answers were right. On comparing with the other chaps afterwards, I discovered that only about half my answers corresponded with those arrived at by the majority of us. I had done the working correctly, but I had made a few stupid slips here and there. Hopes for a credit in this subject seemed pretty dim. History, however, I rushed through at high speed, writing pages on every question. I remember there was a question on the Indian Mutiny which I tore into with gusto, because only the night before I had read about it in detail, anticipating just such a question. French, of course, and Memory Drawing melted away before me. Mere child's play. My diary says that I "did fairly well" in *The Acts* which probably means that I had not fared so successfully. In Geometry, too, I noted that I had done "fairly well" which I know for certain was equivalent to "extremely and disastrously bad". *The Tempest* got a "fairly well", too, and so did *St. Matthew*. Bacon's Essays and Algebra both secured a "fair".

On the 21st July, I remarked: "It has finished. Reading, football and stamp-collecting start in full swing." On the afternoon of that very day, from one to four o'clock, I had done the last subject—Painting. A water-colour sketch of a silver teapot and three or four mangoes arranged on a table. I was the only one to take this subject.

Unlike the year before, I did not plunge completely into an orgy of reading, however. I mixed things this time. I began to write a long story. And I kept up learning my French and German. I also did a lot of painting. And I made up my monthly meteorological charts, noting the temperature graph and working out the "average daily temperature". And on the 8th of August I went to my first dance—an Ice Cream Matinee, as it was called in those days. It was held at "Rosedale". I drank three rum punches, and blundered my way through every dance. I created a sensation among the old hands who wondered what phenomenon this could be. A mere schoolboy in shorts only a few months ago attempting to dance the Charleston—and, yes, even the Black Bottom!

Chapter Twenty-four

A PAUCITY OF GODFATHERS

IN NOVEMBER I learnt that the examiners had not liked my attempt to flout their request for an essay. They failed me in English Composition. Perhaps, too, they had thought it presumptuous of me to write about the Earth's Surface when they had specified the Earth's Crust. But, to my surprise, I got a credit in Arithmetic, and, as I had expected, I got an even better-than-ordinary credit in Geography. But there was a shock in History. They failed me in this. In French, as usual, I triumphed, and also in Drawing and Painting. I failed disgustingly, as expected, in Geometry and Algebra—and in Shakespeare and Bacon I dropped through. In all, I secured five credits, but failed the examination as a whole because I did not get a pass in English Composition or History.

Out of the whole lot of us who took this examination, only two were successful.

The Authorities considered it a major set-back in the campaign to get me a job in the Civil Service. It had been calculated that I would have stood an excellent chance of getting the post in the Magistrate's Office if I had passed my School Certificate Examination. Not that this alone, however, would have sufficed, and my mother and aunts realised it, too. In those years of stiff competition in every department of endeavour, you needed more than scholastic qualifications to gain a foothold in any office, government or commercial. The ruling factor was a Godfather behind the scenes. My Uncle John was high in the Civil Service—he was by this time already at the top; Comptroller of Customs—and he moved in a wide circle of highly influential friends. It had been easy for him to get his sons into suitable middle-class jobs. Three he got into the Civil Service, and three into big commercial offices in Georgetown. Two daughters also went into the offices of well-established firms. And all this without the benefit of certificates won in school!

Here in New Amsterdam, my father lived his own very limited life of book-keeping at the Town Hall and reading and art at home. He had no cronies at all, no social life whatever, unless an occasional visit to his sisters and brothers at "Rosedale" can be called social life. Every Sunday, without fail, he attended sung Mass and Evensong, and afterwards came into the vestry with another churchwarden to help count the collection. He exchanged a few polite pleasantries with the Rector—then off home to mix his lemonade in his room and retire for the night. Bitter about his chronic stagnation in the Town Clerk's Office, he was unable to find a godfather to sponsor his own promotion. Where was he to look for a godfather to pull strings on my behalf?

Uncle Bertie was in the Civil Service, but as a godfather he was a negative quantity. Dreamy to the point of vacancy, blushing-shy, he continued to nod over his ledgers in the Department of Registry and Deeds at Colony House; his colleagues called him Mass' Bertie, and he was the butt of innumerable jokes; one day they even went so far as to inveigle him into the old Dutch vault where piles of documents are stacked, then shut the door gently after him. He wailed in terror—but not in terror of the dimly lit vault, not in claustrophobic terror. What terrified him was the attractive Indian girl he found himself alone with!

As for Uncle John, he was, for us in New Amsterdam, a legend. Remote and Olympian, he was heard about but never seen. His brothers and sisters referred to him as Johnnie, but everyone else spoke of him as The Major. A stranger discovering unexpectedly that I was a Mittelholzer, would automatically ask: "What relation are you to the Major?" As a boy of eight or thereabouts, I had been taken by my mother to Georgetown to spend a fortnight in the big house at the corner of Camp and Hatfield Streets where my uncle and his family lived. I have seen pictures of him in uniform, but my memory of him is limited to his waxed moustache and his pleasant if rather brusque voice. Definitely a strong character. Nothing dreamy, shy or self-effacing about him. It is possible that he might have helped behind the scenes on my behalf if he had been asked. But who was to ask him? Not my father who saw him perhaps once in seven or eight years, and who, in any case, would have found it "uncomfortable" to broach such a matter. And within recent years my mother had taken a dislike to all my father's people. She manufactured a number of reasons why the Mittelholzers in Georgetown as well as at "Rosedale" in Main Street in the town here had "no use" for her. She has always been a genius at cooking up imaginary hatreds directed against her. So neither could she approach the Major to enlist his help. My aunts probably had never even met him, and, moreover, they, if not actively opposed to the Mittelholzers, remarked frequently that the Leblancs "have nothing to be ashamed of!" their voices silky and high-pitched with innuendo.

At the Magistrate's Office, in the meantime, a colleague of Mr. T——'s—an East Indian—was actively engaged in godfatherly manoeuvres, and before long the news came. The post had been filled—by an East Indian boy who had just left school.

Chapter Twenty-five

"SIEG ODER TOD!"

WHEN THE church-bells were ringing, the whistles blowing and the carbide bombs booming, I sat at the dining-table writing. I was writing my first serious story. 1927 and my schooldays were behind me. This story was no blood-and-thunder adventure influenced by what I had seen in the film-serials. It was sober, realistic everyday life. I cannot remember anything about the plot, but there were only two characters—a man and his son—and it was called *The Doubloon*. I completed it the following day, the first of January, 1928—even without referring to my diary I recall that. It was a short-story of about three thousand words. And I did something I had never before done. I asked my father to read it and give me his opinion. He did so—and his opinion was favourable. He was quite pleased.

On the seventh of the month I also did something that I had never before done. I sent the story to an editor for consideration. The Editor of *Pearson's Magazine*. The first shot in the Battle had been fired. Or it might be better to amend that and say the first shot in the first battle. For I had made up my mind that this was it. I had to be a writer. That was what I wanted to do in life. Write stories and books. It must be my career. I mentioned this casually to my father and he smiled and shook his head. "You can't make a living out of writing," he said. "That requires experience."

That sounded a bit odd, and for a long time afterwards I pondered on it. Did he mean I required experience of writing before I could succeed? Well, in that case, surely the only thing was for me to go straight ahead and *write*. You can only gain experience of a thing by doing it. Much long afterwards it occurred to me that he might have meant experience of living. In that case there was sound sense in what he had said. But this, I repeat, occurred to me long afterwards. Years afterwards. In that January of 1928 I smiled to myself and filliped his words lightly out of my consciousness. It doesn't matter, I thought, what anyone says. I can do it—and I shall show them I can do it.

So having posted the manuscript of *The Doubloon*—neatly handwritten—to *Pearson's Magazine* on the 7th, I sat down and started to write another story on the 12th. I completed it on the 24th, and on the 26th I wrote a short-short (380 words). On the 30th I started to write another, and on the same day posted the manuscript of one of the two already completed to the Editor of *Pearson's Weekly*. The new one I had just started was a long short-story, and it gave me some trouble; I didn't complete it until the 18th of February. And revising it and making a fair copy took me until the 1st of March—and on the day before, the 29th of February, I had received the manuscript of *The Doubloon* back from the Editor of *Pearson's Magazine*. In an accompanying letter, the Editor said that while the story showed promise, it was "too slight for us", and so he regretted that he must return it.

The first repulse. Not a rejection, but a repulse. For in my imagination the whole thing had taken on the flavour of a military campaign. I was a general at the head of an army, and the objectives were clearly defined. The enemy was Life-cum-editors-and-publishers-in-London. I must hurl the whole weight of my war-machine against their defences, infiltrate here, infiltrate there, and then, in one big offensive, batter away at the inner fortifications until victory was achieved. The acceptance of a short short-story by a weekly paper would constitute a mere infiltration; the same would apply to an article. But a full-length story accepted by one of the monthly magazines, like *The Strand*, *Pearson's* or *The Royal*, would be a major break-through. Final victory would be represented by the acceptance of a novel by a publisher.

So on the 1st of March I posted the story just completed (a 7,000-word story) to the Editor of *Pearson's Magazine*, and on the 8th I began writing another.

Exactly two calendar months before—on the 8th of January—I went on the *stelling* (the wharf, when translated from the

Dutch) to see J.P. off on the ferry-boat. His parents had decided that he must take another shot at the School Certificate—and they had arranged for him to become a pupil of Queen's College in Georgetown. The era of our strolls and discussions and arguments, the era of the Nut Pyramids and Nelson Lees, was behind us—at least, for the time being. His objective was dentistry, and so it was essential that he should continue at school.

The Authorities raised no objection to my being at home engaged in my writing. They could suggest no alternative. No rumours of other Government vacancies had reached them, and my mother had always viewed with nightmare abhorrence the idea of my working in a shop, so no feelers were made in the direction of the managers of any big shops. An office would have been all right, of course, but jobs in commercial offices were as difficult to get as those in the Civil Service—and a godfather was just as necessary.

For recreation, I went on trying to play soccer, and I still read an odd Nelson Lee and Sexton Blake, though *Pearson's Magazine* and novels featured a lot in my reading now. And I still served at the altar, and held the Rector's cope in processions.

On the 10th of April, I received from the Editor of *Pearson's Magazine* the story I had posted to him on the 1st of March. But never mind! I sent it off the same day to the Editor of *Cassell's Magazine*. And I began revising a story completed only two or three days before.

The battle must go on. Throw in more reserves.

J.P. came home for the holidays, and he did not fail to remark the new war language I had coined. He uttered mocking chuckles. If we went for a stroll and I fell silent for any length of time, he would ask: "Why so quiet, Barno? Hearing the heavy artillery?"

There was not much of the clown in me these days. The brooding part of me began to predominate. The situation that faced me was too serious for frivolity. Every time I looked in the newspaper and saw that a ship was due from England, I had to steel myself for an enemy onslaught. When I heard the postman dismount from his bicycle at the gateway, I knew it was Zero Hour. The bulky envelopes meant another repulse.

Disheartening, but that was war. Attack again. Back went the manuscripts to other editors. Sometimes three or four went off at the same time, for I never stopped writing in the intervals of waiting to hear about those despatched.

No one guessed what a grim struggle was being waged. I presented a blank face to the outside world. I went to soccer matches as a spectator, played in some matches when I was picked. I went to ice-cream matinees—the functions that began at five in the afternoon and went on until midnight—and danced as though I were a carefree young man not yet settled in any special occupation. Only I could hear the artillery booming in the background, sometimes drowning out the wailing of the saxophone and the cling-clang of the piano.

Early in August, I met Holly L——, a girl from Demerara come to New Amsterdam for the day. I fell for her at sight, and began to bombard her with quotations of an appropriate nature taken from *As You Like It.* It was a major infatuation, but I took it all in my stride; it did not impede the war effort.

I took part in a revue. I had to sing in the chorus with about eight or ten other chaps, and an equal number of girls. *Me and Jane in a plane* and *Side by Side* were the numbers we had to sing. I enjoyed it—but in a detached way. I enjoyed nothing wholeheartedly now. The noise of battle was too distracting—or too absorbing, perhaps—to permit any pleasurable occupation to seem more than a trivial diversion. The Objective had to be kept perpetually in view. The Vision must flame bright day and night. No relaxing. Plan and plot. Attack and counter-attack.

The Daily Chronicle, one of the local newspapers, published a short short-story I wrote in July—my diary describes it as "paltry"—and it was the first thing of my own I had seen in print. But I didn't even count it as an infiltration. The local papers were of no interest to me so far as my main objective was concerned. Their standards were too low.

Apart from that "paltry" effort, I wrote seventeen stories during 1928, and sent them off to English editors—and had them all returned, one, two, three at a time, as the case might be. A gradual snowball effect was building up, for I was not prepared to discard a manuscript simply because one or two editors had turned it down. I had to send it to a third and fourth, even a fifth. More and more began to go off at the same time. And more and more began to return by the same post. Massed attacks. And massed repulses.

But morale continued high, and in January, 1929, I started on my first novel. It was to be a grand offensive. A powerful build-up of forces, and one swift thrust that would smash the enemy's defences and inflict such heavy punishment on him that victory would be certain.

On the 1st of March I completed *The Terrible Four*, a story of tremendous originality—situation, characters, plot and style—and had no doubt that this would carry the day. The setting was a network of caves behind the great waterfall, Kaieteur, in the interior of the colony (caves do exist behind this fall), and four men, an Englishman, a German, a Frenchman and a Spaniard, each an eccentric who had become tired of civilisation, had banded together and decided to cut themselves off from the world. They established their own community within the caves behind the fall, inviting others tired like themselves to join them in their troglodyte existence. Peculiar orgies and ceremonies took place, and all was going well until two people, a young man and his fiancée, arrived. They were not tired enough, and objected to much of what they saw, so they were made prisoners. The rest of the story described their attempts to escape and the eventual fate of the whole community.

It was a bulky script, and I had to send it by parcel post. It went to George Newnes on the 6th of March. And then I settled down to doing more short stories, and even some articles of a humorous sort to be hurled against such papers as *The Passing Show* and *The Humorist*. I wrote a 600-word thing in serious vein, which I thought might interest *The Connoisseur*. I sent it off, and it was accepted—the first acceptance by an English editor. I got for it a guinea and a half. (*The Daily Chronicle* had paid me nothing at all for the story they published).

After a build-up of hopes throughout the next three months, the letter arrived from George Newnes on the 19th of June. It was kind and encouraging, and written by a Mr. Pollock, if my memory is not faulty—and I think not. It was a longish letter, and said that the story showed a great deal of promise, but that I still had a lot to learn about construction. It advised me, too, to study the prose of George Moore, Walter Pater and H. G. Wells. Regretfully the manuscript was being returned under separate cover. (By the same post came two stories, returned by the Editor of *Pearson's Magazine*).

My diary comments on the following day: "Trying to feel bright."

Off went *The Terrible Four* to Hodder and Stoughton! Off went more stories to the editors! No retreat. At all costs the enemy lines must be breached . . . On the 16th of August *The Terrible Four* came back from Hodder and Stoughton . . . "Never say surrender!" says my diary. Off went the script to Hutchinson's. On the following day, I started writing another novel. Another offensive must be prepared . . . "Registered," says my diary, "six stories to Editor *Strand Magazine*." Throw in more reserves . . . "Finished Chapter Fifteen." That was on the 10th of September. On the 17th the *Wide World* returned an article. On the 18th "re-wrote and posted short story to *Punch*." On the 21st "started and finished Chapter Twenty-four." Posted article to *My Weekly* on the 25th. After starting and finishing Chapter Twenty-eight on the 26th, I noted "a touch of brain fag." But I went on to write Chapter Twenty-nine the following day. On the 4th of October the last chapter was finished, on the 15th *Fate versus George Forbes* was launched against Hodder and Stoughton. On the 29th the Editor of *The Strand* returned the six stories, so off they went on the same day to *The Royal Magazine*. Throw in more reserves. No retreat. Victory goes to the strong and the persistent. Ignore the taunts on the home front. Keep on throwing in more reserves. The enemy defences *must* be smashed. The order of the day went out to the troops:

"Victory or death!"

APPENDICES

I

Had I been an adult in 1909, the year of my birth, it is just possible that I might have felt the disadvantage of my swarthy complexion, for at that time complexion was sometimes a barrier to advancement, especially in the Civil Service or in big commercial firms: and that is, advancement right to the top. My maternal grandfather, for instance, acted as Post-master General but could not be confirmed in this post purely on account of his complexion—swarthy like mine. Yet it must be pointed out that racial prejudice in British Guiana, even in those days, was not an outright fact. The colony was too British in spirit by then (a century of continuous British rule had already elapsed), and the polite hypocrisy of the British forbade any public display of prejudice.

Further, the pure whites were (and still are) a very small minority, and simply could not afford to show open discrimination or practise any unpleasant form of segregation.

Indeed, sad to relate, it was my own class—people of coloured admixture but of fair or olive complexions—who dispensed any colour snobbery that it was possible to dispense. It was my class which looked down upon the East Indian sugar plantation labourers ("coolies" we called them, whether they were labourers or eventually became doctors or barristers or Civil Servants). It was my class which considered the Portuguese social inferiors because of their background of door-to-door peddling, rum-shops, salt-goods shops and pawn-shops and their low standards of living. We, too, treated the Chinese sweet-sellers and shopkeepers with condescension because of their poor-immigrant status. We even looked with a certain distinct aloofness upon the young Englishmen who came out to serve as sugar-plantation overseers. We deemed them "white riff-raff". And as for the negroes, it goes without saying that they were serving people; that was an accepted tradition dating from Slavery days.

Only the pure-blooded whites could discriminate adversely

against me and my class, and it would have been very awkward for them if they had tried to do so, for they were too heavily dependent upon all the other social elements beneath them. The most they could do was to keep to themselves in their own tight, tiny group: in their homes and in their clubs. They had to mix with everyone else in church, school, cinema, town-hall and on every public occasion.

2

To someone who has never visited British Guiana, the word "creek" might prove misleading. Rivers are such giant streams in this part of the world that any natural water-course less than a quarter of a mile wide at its mouth is generally dubbed a creek. The Canje Creek, for instance, is over a hundred miles long, and, even in its higher reaches, seldom narrower than fifty yards. In any other country this would count as an important river, but when judged alongside the mother river, the Berbice, it appears a mere trickle. The Berbice is two and a half miles wide at its mouth, and is over four hundred miles long. The Essequibo is so wide at its mouth that there are large cultivated islands in its estuary. You cannot see across from one bank to the other at this point. It is six hundred miles long.

3

"Mass' " is an abbreviation of the old "Massa" used in Slavery days. The use of this term of address, when I was a boy, had become extremely specialised. In Slavery days it was used by the slaves in addressing any male member of the family, but in my time only boys were thus addressed. The head of the family had become "sir".

When the term is used by a member of the middle-class, either as a form of address or of reference, towards a member of his own class it is generally done in derision, the implication being that such an individual cannot be treated as an adult but must be patronised in a manner befitting an adolescent. Hence "Mass' Bertie".

4

The Esplanade in New Amsterdam was in the nature of a park. It was a grassy strip of land bordering the mudflats of the river estuary, and sheltered by huge saman trees. The bandstand stood at a point about midway along its length. The road ran on its eastern side, and to the west loomed the waste of *courida* bushes that extended for about a quarter of a mile down to the mudflats and the muddy water of the river estuary.